Battlegrou

OPERATION MA

THE ISLAND

Battleground Europe
OPERATION MARKET GARDEN

THE ISLAND
Nijmegen to Arnhem September 1944

Tim Saunders

LEO COOPER

Dedicated to my daughter
Victoria Saunders
with Love

Other books in the series by Tim Saunders
Hill 112 – Normandy
Hell's Highway – Market Garden
Nijmegen – Market Garden
Gold Beach-JIG – Normandy

Published by
LEO COOPER
an imprint of
Pen & Sword Books Limited
47 Church Street, Barnsley, South Yorkshire S70 2AS
Copyright © Tim Saunders, 2002

ISBN 0 85052 861 5

A CIP catalogue of this book is available
from the British Library

Printed by Redwood Books Limited
Trowbridge, Wiltshire

For up-to-date information on other titles produced under the Leo Cooper
imprint, please telephone or write to:
Pen & Sword Books Ltd, FREEPOST, 47 Church Street
Barnsley, South Yorkshire S70 2AS
Telephone 01226 734222

CONTENTS

Infantrymen of the Dorsets clearing a bunker built into a dyke on the Island. A rare action photograph.

ACKNOWLEDGEMENTS

I am indebted to veterans and inhabitants of the Island, particularly those of 43rd Wessex Division, for their help with this book. Much has been written over the sixty years since the dramatic events of September 1944. However, some of the material has proved to be superficial, contradictory and often simply incorrect but veterans' contributions and examination of archives has helped clear up a number of myths. Again, I am indebted to the hard-pressed staff of British regimental headquarters, whose forebears' battles are covered in this book. They have been most helpful; regimental secretaries and knowledgeable volunteers are a mine of information. Across the Atlantic, veterans associations have helped me with official and personal accounts. Visits to the Public Record Office and archives of airborne museums in Britain and Holland were essential and I unreservedly thank them for their help.

I would also like to thank the many Dutch people who helped me locate and gain access to some of the more obscure sites. It would take too long to name them here but their greatest contribution has been their warmth and friendliness. Sources in Germany, have helped guide me to records of *Wehrmacht* and *Luftwaffe* units, including to some of the many *ad hoc* formations and units taking part in the fighting on the Island.

Again, I am indebted to both family and friends for their tolerant support and encouragement, while I researched and wrote this book. I am most grateful for the time they spent spotting errors and inconsistencies, while reading drafts of the manuscript. Thank you one and all.

Maps

The Dutch maps recommended for exploring this series of actions are the Nederland 1:50,000 scale. They are readily available at shops in Arnhem and Nijmegen. Sheet 40 West covers the main Island battles and Sheet 39 Ost the battles at Opheusden and Randwijk.

INTRODUCTION

This is the third volume in *Battleground Europe's* MARKET GARDEN series, taking over the story following 82nd US Airborne's epic crossing of the Waal and the Guards Armoured Division's charge across the Nijmegen Road Bridge. These events are covered in the *Battleground* titles *Nijmegen* and *Hell's Highway*. This volume covers the fighting, during late September and early October 1944, over ten miles of flat boggy polder land between the River Waal at Nijmegen and the Rhine at Arnhem. The drained countryside is properly called the Betwe, but was known to the Allies as the 'Island'.

The Island like much of Holland, is flat and low, but the Island is particularly so. Both sides complained that the only areas of high ground were the broad earth dykes, rising over twenty feet from the surrounding countryside. Built to contain two of Europe's mighty rivers, the dykes provide the only vantage points on the Island, other than churches and mills. However, north of the Rhine, German-held high ground dominated virtually the whole of the Island. At ground level, the Island's many orchards and belts of trees gave generally short fields of fire, especially around villages. Not only was it difficult to find positions from which it was possible to engage the enemy at any significant range, but trenches and foxholes had to be less than three feet deep due to the high water table. The numerous trees also meant that infantry positions needed overhead cover to protect occupants from wounds caused by shells bursting in the treetops and hurling down wooden splinters. During the day, movement on the Island attracted shellfire, therefore, resupply and relief-in-place was carried out at night. Other than the main Nijmegen to Arnhem highway, the roads on the Island were designed for light farming traffic and could not take sustained movement by tanks and heavily laden vehicles, and soon started to break up.

Over the years, attention has been focused on the 'highlight' events at Nijmegen and Arnhem but this is to sideline events that are important for a proper understanding of MARKET GARDEN as a whole. The extent to which XXX Corps's artillery helped preserve the Oosterbeek Perimeter and the factors behind the crossings of the 1st Polish Airborne and 4th Dorsets and the eventual evacuation are seldom fully examined.

On the morning of 21 September 1944, just ten miles lay between the Allies at the Nijmegen Bridge and the remains of 1st British Airborne Division, confined in the Oosterbeek Perimeter. The battle fought by 2 PARA to hold the northern end of the Arnhem bridge was already over, with the paratroopers having fought for sixty-eight hours against

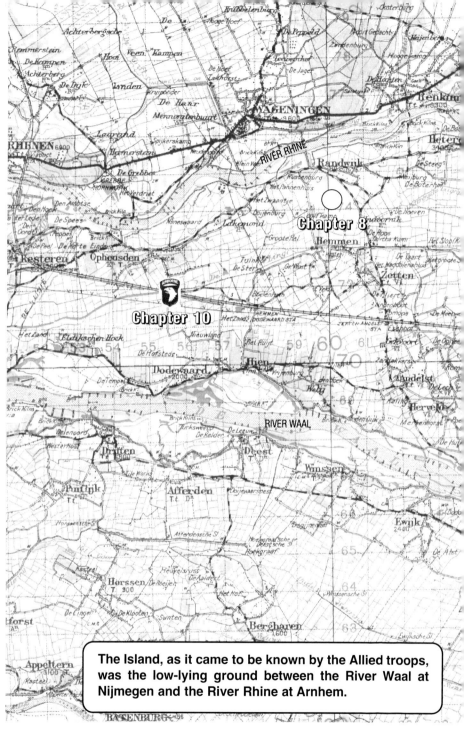

Chapter 8

Chapter 10

RIVER RHINE

RIVER WAAL

The Island, as it came to be known by the Allied troops, was the low-lying ground between the River Waal at Nijmegen and the River Rhine at Arnhem.

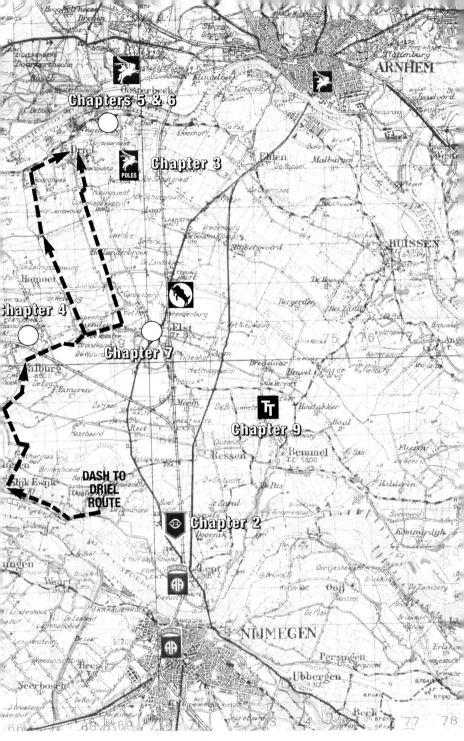

Chapters 5 & 6

Chapter 3

POLES

Chapter 4

Chapter 7

Elst

Chapter 9

TT

DASH TO
DRIEL
ROUTE

Chapter 2

ARNHEM

HUISSEN

Bemmel

Ressen

NIJMEGEN

Ubbergen

Beek

mounting odds, after a heroic battle. However, XXX Corps's attempts to reach the Rhine must be seen against the background of a 'pencil thin corridor' being repeatedly cut behind them, starving units of combat supplies and reinforcements. The exaggerated expectations of XXX Corps by some commentators, in these circumstances, are highly questionable. However, credit is due to the Germans, who displayed an ability to mount effective defences with *ad hoc* formations, made up of units and individuals, who had escaped from the fortresses along the North Sea coast. The failure to secure the sixty-mile Scheldt waterway between Antwerp and the sea, across which the Germans escaped, was a grievous error.

As a final point, it should be explained that the principal memorials in the battle area are covered in the tour notes. However, space does not permit the inclusion of every military and liberation memorial on the Island. But most can be found in town centres or at the scene of the action described in the text.

I hope this book will encourage those studying MARKET GARDEN to visit and appreciate the largely overlooked battles fought to open the road across the Island to Arnhem.

At home or on the ground, enjoy the tour.

TJJS, LICHFIELD

The maroon silk Arnhem Banner presented to 4 Dorset by 1st Airborne Division to commemorate their crossing into the Oosterbeek Perimeter and the award of the Battle Honour 'Arnhem'. 4 Dorset were the only non-airborne unit to cross the Rhine during Operation MARKET GARDEN.

CHAPTER ONE

MARKET GARDEN – Background and Plan

'Monty's plan was one of the most imaginative of the war.'
General Omar Bradley

In September 1944, after the resounding defeat of the Germans in Normandy, described by an Allied intelligence officer as being:

'... a blood-bath big enough even for their extravagant tastes, that has brought the end of the war in Europe within sight, almost within reach.'

Consequently, it seemed reasonable to expect that the war would be over by Christmas. With the Allied commanders competing for the limited logistic resources to reach the Rhine and Germany, Field Marshal Montgomery proposed a daring operation. He outlined a plan to General Eisenhower, in which, he proposed to lay 'a carpet of airborne troops' across Holland, over which XXX Corps would drive from the Belgian border to the Zuider Zee, cutting off German North Sea garrisons. The Allies would then envelop the Ruhr and strike east towards Berlin. However, the Supreme Commander, who was for largely political reasons, following a broad front strategy, could not allocate full logistic priority to Montgomery. Eisenhower was unable to sustain even half of his Armies on active operations from the Normandy beaches. Consequently, giving Montgomery's narrow front to Berlin priority, to the detriment of Patton's Third Army, would never have been acceptable. By this stage in the campaign, America was the Alliance's leading partner and US public opinion was a determining factor in Anglo-American relations.

Believing that he had logistic priority and knowing that Eisenhower would have to reinforce success, Montgomery upgraded earlier plans for divisional airborne operation (COMET) into the corps level MARKET GARDEN. Operation MARKET, was the parachute and glider landings by the three airborne divisions allocated to Lieutenant General FAM 'Boy' Browning's 1st British Airborne Corps. 101st US Airborne Division was to secure canal bridges and twenty miles of road north of Eindhoven. 82nd 'All American' US Airborne Division was to secure the major river crossings of the Maas at Grave and the Waal in the city of Nijmegen. The third Allied airborne division, 1st British, was to drop on heaths well to the west of their objective – the Arnhem

Bridges across the Rhine. The airborne plans were less than perfect, as far as the soldiers were concerned. The Drop Zones (DZs), miles away from the objectives, were dictated by the airforces, who in what were perceived to be the last days of the war, were unwilling to accept potentially high flak casualties to aircraft or aircrew. Major General Sosabowski, commander of the 1st Independent Polish Parachute Brigade, wrote of the Arnhem DZs:

'We had lost the one indispensable element an airborne operation needs: surprise! Any fool of a German would immediately know our plans.'

For instance, it would be at least five hours before the Arnhem bridges could be taken. Secondly, despite the huge investment in transport aircraft, only half of the Airborne Corps could be delivered into battle in the first drop. Compounding this, was a lack of US ground crew, which led to a decision that there would only be one drop per day. In addition, vital troops were needed to secure DZs and glider landing zones. Consequently, only a minority were available to take key objectives on day one, as the airborne divisions would arrive over three days. It would have made all the difference if the Airborne Corps had been able to arrive in a 'Single clap of thunder'.

Accusations have been made that the MARKET GARDEN plan was arrived at by virtually ignoring the 'enemy' in the formal appreciation of the day. During early September 1944, some remarkably accurate intelligence painted an unfavourable picture for airborne troops who were to be dropped sixty miles behind the German front line:

'... it is reported that one of the broken panzer divisions has been sent back to the area north of Arnhem to rest and refit; this might produce some fifty tanks.'

A 1st Airborne Division intelligence summary dated 7 September followed:

'The present tank strength is about 250 tanks. The maximum that can be expected in the way of reinforcements is 350, with a possible 15,000 troops, making a total strength in panzer troops of 600 tanks and 60,000 men.'

This was the remnant of the elite II SS Panzer *Korps,* withdrawn to re-equip following the retreat from Normandy. However, this information was, in the all-pervading enthusiasm to get into battle, ignored by Montgomery, HQ 2nd Army and both the Airborne Corps HQ and 1st Airborne Division. On hearing the original Operation COMET plan, Polish General Sosabowski blurted out 'But the Germans, General, the Germans' and by the time the MARKET GARDEN PLAN was

September 1944, after [thr]ee months of heavy [figh]ting, France had been [lib]erated, along with much [of] Belgium. The German [arm]y had fallen back to its [ow]n national borders and [the] Allied forces were [po]ised for a thrust into [Hit]ler's Third Reich itself.

GERMANY

HOLLAND

Arnhem
Nijmegen
Munster
Wesel
Essen
Eindhoven
R. Rhine

4 September
BRUSSELS
GERMANY
Maastricht
Aachen
Cologne
3 September Liège
17 September
ARMY GROUP B
ARMY GROUP
Mainz
R. Mosel
LUX.
GERMANY

BELGIUM

[Be]lgian [Ar]my

[Brit]ish [A]rmy

[U]S [Fir]st [Arm]y

Reims
R. Marne
R. Meuse
Metz
4 September
Nancy

[U]S [3]rd [Arm]y

26 August

French 1st Army

US 7th Army

General Eisenhower

General Montgomery

Lieutenant General Crerar
Canadian 1st Army

Lieutenant General Dempsey
British 2nd Army

Lieutenant General Bradley
US 1st Army

Lieutenant General Patton
US 3rd Army

General Lattre de Tassigny
French 1st Army

General Patch
US 7th Army

presented, the enemy were almost totally ignored as a planning factor. When shown air photographs of panzers in the woods near Arnhem, General Browning retorted 'I wouldn't trouble myself about these if I were you... they're probably not serviceable at any rate'. Famously, intelligence officers who raised the issue of the German armour, were visited by medical officers for a 'chat' and others sent on leave. So complete was the cognitive dissonance amongst commanders that they would sideline anyone who did not share their delusions. They

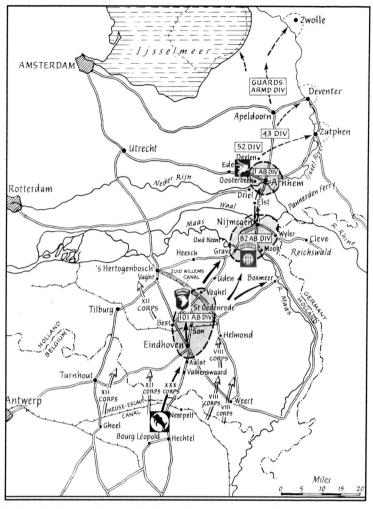

believed that the future of airborne forces was at stake.

Operation GARDEN was the land part of the battle, which was to be executed by Lieutenant General Horrocks's XXX Corps. Their drive north, spearheaded by the Guard's Armoured Division, was predicated on an assumption that there would be little serious opposition. However, the Allied advance from Normandy had been slowing as it crossed Belgium and the seven day halt on the Escaut Canal had enabled the Germans to bring some sort of order to their defences in Holland.

In summary, the compromises and false assumptions made during a very short planning period, led to heroic fighting by paratroopers and XXX Corps, as well as self sacrifice by many valiant aircrews over the eight days of MARKET GARDEN.

Hell's Highway

On the morning of Sunday 17 September 1944 the Guards Armoured Division was ready to break out of the Neerpelt Bridgehead, which a week earlier the Irish Guards had secured across the Escaut Canal, to form the MARKET GARDEN springboard. As General Horrocks waited on a factory roof, a coded radio message arrived confirming that the airborne operation was on. At 1435 hours, he watched as an artillery barrage fell on the pencil straight road to Valkenswaard and the Irish Guards began the sixty-mile advance to Arnhem. However, having allowed the Guards' tanks into their position the Germans ambushed them knocking out nine Shermans. The barrage had to be repeated and, supported by RAF Typhoons, the Guards drove on to Valkenswaard, which they reached at last light. Here the Irish Guards were halted for the night. They had been due to reach the 101st Airborne Division at Eindhoven and cross the Son

XXX Corps trucks crossing the Grave Bridge after its capture by the 101st Airborne.

Bridge that evening but the Screaming Eagles had also failed to reach Eindhoven.

Despite 'the best drop ever', 101st Airborne were unable to take the vital Son Bridge intact, when it was blown up in the face of 506 Parachute Infantry Regiment (PIR). Improvising a footbridge, the Americans resumed the advance to Eindhoven the following morning, where they met the Guards. On the night of 18/19 September Allied engineers built a Bailey Bridge across the canal at Son and early the following morning, Grenadier Guards' tanks led the British drive north

SS-Brigadeführer Heinz Harmel's 10th SS Frundsberg Panzer Division, a part of the II SS Panzer Korps, was re-fitting in the Arnhem area, following the heavy fighting in Normandy.

up the single road. Within two hours, they had reached the 82nd Airborne at the Grave Bridge. It seemed reasonable to expect that they would soon reach Arnhem but this was only the conclusion of the first phase of the battle for what became known as 'Hell's Highway'.

The Germans recovered from the surprise attack and directed *ad hoc* 'divisions' towards Hell's Highway. They attacked the Allied columns in attempts to cut the lifeline to the airborne and British armour to the north. Major General Maxwell Taylor, commanding the 101st Airborne Division described the nature of the battle and his scheme of manoeuvre:

SS-Gruppenführer William Bittrich, commander of II SS Panzer Korps.

'We were forced to spread along the highway, garrisoning key towns with the hope of being able to move rapidly to meet hostile thrusts before they could become dangerous. When the enemy was close enough to the road to become dangerous to the traffic on it, he had to be fought and destroyed; on the periphery of this vital zone it was a matter of nice judgement to decide how to discourage the enemy from attacking without becoming involved in a serious engagement.'

In this aim, General Taylor was only partly successful, as the route was cut no less than five times. The Germans were successful in denying the Allies a consistent flow of combat supplies to the troops fighting across the Island to the Rhine. The 101st had a difficult task, as increasingly weary paratroopers marched and counter marched to clear successive threats to and actual cuts of Hell's Highway. The full story of the part played by 101st Airborne and the Guards Armoured Divisions, in this area is covered in the **Battleground** volume *Hell's Highway*.

General Horrocks, commander of XXX Corps given the task of reaching the British 1st Airborne at Arnhem.

The Capture of the Nijmegen Bridges

The Operation MARKET mission allocated to 82nd Airborne Division was very different. They had to seize bridges across two of Europe's major rivers, the Maas and the Waal and hold the vital Groesbeek Heights on the very borders of Germany. Controversially, the 82nd had been denied a *coup de main* against the vital Nijmegen Road Bridge, because of fears of heavy aircraft casualties from the German flak guns defending the Waal crossings. Following some confusion, 1/508 PIR only moved to take the bridge after the Germans had reinforced the small Nijmegen garrison. The delay meant that the American paratroopers arrived in the city at the same time as elements of 9th SS *Hohenstaufen* Panzer Division, who checked their advance. The failure on the evening of 17 September condemned the Allies to a costly three-day battle to take the Nijmegen Bridges.

With the arrival of the Guards on 19 September, a joint Anglo-American attack was mounted on the bridges. With the situation in Arnhem becoming increasingly desperate, two armoured columns rushed the bridges. However, the Germans had reinforced their

Nijmegen Bridge under new management, 21 September 1944, courtesy of the 82nd Airborne and Guards Armoured Division.

Schwerepunkt at Nijmegen and the Allied attack failed. On 20 September, the Allies mounted a deliberate attack. While 3rd Battalion 504 PIR carried out a heroic assault river crossing of the Waal to outflank the Germans, which was described as 'unbelievable' by watching British commanders. The attack was a success and at nightfall, American paratroopers and Grenadier Guards' tanks met at the Bridge's northern end.

Following success, came inactivity. Commanders of 504 PIR were furious but while they had been fighting their battle, the situation in the rear had deteriorated sharply. Not only had 107 Panzer Brigade cut Hell's Highway, for a second time but also the American positions on Groesbeek Heights were under severe pressure from *Korps Feldt*. Thus, enemy action was not only delaying vital combat supplies for the Guards' tanks but also taking commanders' attention and reserves away from the Island and the road to Arnhem. The full story of the epic battle for the Bridges is told in the **Battleground Europe** title *Nijmegen*.

Lieutenant General Browning

Arnhem

Lieutenant General 'Boy' Browning had allocated the most dangerously exposed task to 1st British Airborne Division; the capture of the Arnhem Bridges some sixty miles behind the enemy lines. The British Paras admitted that they were beginning to refer to themselves as 'First Stillborne Division', following the cancellation of successive operations. Candidly, Major Geoffrey Powell admitted to being 'gung-ho' and 'desperate to get into action before the end of the war'. So keen were they, that they ignored evidence of the remains of *Obergruppenführer* Willi Bittrich's II SS Panzer *Korps* in the woods north of Arnhem.

Of the three airborne divisions, 1st Division had its plans most radically shaped by airforce considerations. Their DZs were no less than eight miles from their objectives in Arnhem. Witnessing the drop himself, *Generalfeldmarshall* Model lost no time in confirming Bittrich's orders to his *Korps* to counter-attack and deny the bridge at Nijmegen. Despite the 'lightening reaction of the Germans', and the presence of SS troops training in the woods between the DZs and Arnhem, 2 PARA reached the northern end of the Bridge. 1 and 3 PARA's approach was blocked and 1st Airlanding Brigade had to hold the landing grounds for the following days' lifts.

On 18 and 19 September the battle in Arnhem to reach 2 PARA continued but with the SS soldiers of the *Hohenstaufen* occupying vantage points in buildings and on high ground, the attacks failed. Meanwhile, 4th Parachute Brigade had been halted near their DZs. 1st Airborne Division started to fall back into a defensive perimeter at Oosterbeek, leaving 2 PARA isolated at the northern end of the Bridge. All hope was pinned on the swift arrival of XXX Corps.

Also under command of the 1st Airborne Division, was 1st Polish Independent Parachute Brigade. General Sosbawoski had severe reservations about the operation and to make matters worse his brigade was planned to land in two separate lifts on different DZs/LZs. The Brigade's twenty-five gliders were to land on LZ L on D+2, with the parachute element dropping on the Island, south of the Arnhem on DZ K. The landing on LZ L was chaotic and coincided with an attack by 9th SS Panzer Division. To make matters worse, the Poles and soldiers of 7 Kings Own Scottish Border Regiment became involved in a messy firefight in which they shot each other up. Scheduled to jump somewhat later, the Polish parachute element's drop was cancelled, as the weather deteriorated and was not to arrive for another three days.

The battle on the Island to reach the Rhine at Arnhem, ten miles away, began on the morning of 21 September. However, with bridges on Hell's Highway damaged, with heavy traffic attempting to use a single exposed route and the Germans far more numerous and aggressive than estimated, XXX Corps was behind schedule. General Horrocks had hoped to reach Arnhem in just forty-eight to seventy-two hours but the operation had already taken three and a half days. MARKET GARDEN always had a slim margin of error and the initial stages of the battle had seen setbacks but with the capture of the Nijmegen Bridges, there was still a chance of success.

THE ROAD TO ARNHEM – 21 SEPTEMBER 1944

'The line of communication must be certain and well established, for every army that acts from a distant base and is not careful to keep this line perfectly open marches upon a precipice. It moves to certain ruin if the road by which provisions, ammunition, and reinforcements are to be brought up is not entirely secured.'

Raimundo Montecuccoli (1609 - 80)
Memoroe della guerra ed instruzione d'un general (Venice 1703)

Having seized the bridges across the Waal in a daring Anglo-American operation, Lieutenant General Horrocks was unable to exploit the success. However, he had anticipated the need for an infantry division to take over the lead across the flat, boggy country of the Island. 43rd Wessex Infantry Division were ordered forward to take the lead. However, as Horrocks explained:

'I did not realize at this time that they were so badly blocked on that one "blasted" road which was constantly under fire and so often cut. In many cases, the front line of 101st Division was the ditch on the side of the road. The administrative situation at this time was deteriorating rapidly, and artillery ammunition, like almost everything else, was beginning to be in short supply.'

Field Marshall Montgomery talking to Major General G. I. Thomas of 43rd Wessex Division, watched by General Horrocks.

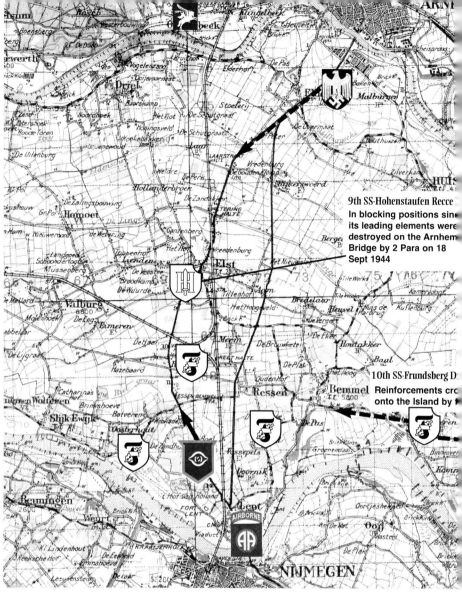

9th SS-Hohenstaufen Recce
In blocking positions sin
its leading elements were
destroyed on the Arnhem
Bridge by 2 Para on 18
Sept 1944

10th SS-Frundsberg D
Reinforcements crc
onto the Island by 1

In addition, as has already been mentioned, 82nd Airborne Division was under attack from the south-east (effectively its rear) and the Guards had been committed to heavy fighting and were low on ammunition. With little remaining tank ammunition and with the infantry of the Irish Guards Group reduced to the equivalent of just five platoons, they could not immediately resume battle with even a forlorn hope of success. Meanwhile, on the Island, SS *Brigadeführer* Heinz Harmel was bringing forward every available soldier, anti-tank weapon and tank to block the road north to Arnhem. Disturbing reports of enemy armoured movement on the Island flowed into the various Allied headquarters. Also, Sergeant Peter Robinson, who had led the Grenadier Guards' heroic armoured charge across the Nijmegen Bridge, confirmed the presence of anti-tank guns covering the road, just beyond the railway underpass, to the north of Lent. Without the fresh infantry of 43rd Wessex Division, overnight General Horrocks could not continue the advance to Arnhem – much to the fury of the 82nd Airborne Division, who felt that their sacrifices on the Waal had been in vain.

The terrain that the spearhead of XXX Corps now had to cross, was worse than anything experienced so far. General Horrocks summed up the military qualities of the ground:

> *'With its dykes, high embankments carrying the road and deep ditches on either side it was most unsuitable for armoured warfare. It was perfect defensive country in which the anti-tank gun hidden in the orchard was always master of the tank silhouetted against the skyline.'*

With the weather deteriorating daily, ground conditions on the Island would get worse.

The Guards Attack – AM Thursday 21 September 1944

The following day, with 43rd Division halted on Hell's Highway, General Horrocks had no choice but to task the depleted Guards Armoured Division to attempt to reach Arnhem, up a very exposed road that they knew to be covered by anti-tank fire. The Coldstream Guards Group were fighting with the 82nd on the Groesbeek Heights and the Welsh Guards were holding the Grave Bridge, only the Grenadiers and Irish Guards were available to exploit success. The Grenadiers were, however, badly disorganised and greatly reduced in strength after two days of battle in Nijmegen and the tanks of the Irish Guards were virtually out of ammunition. The only troops available were the depleted infantry of 3 Irish Guards, organized into three weak companies. On the night of 20/21 September, Numbers 2 and 4 Companies crossed the Nijmegen Bridge onto the Island to thickened up the positions held by the widely scattered 504 PIR. The Irish Guard's regimental historian records the busy night:

> *'Sporadic fighting continued far into the night on both banks and on the bridge itself SS soldiers in the girders snipped the Sappers who were removing the demolition charges. The Guardsmen shot these snipers*

down like rooks, all except those who had lashed themselves to the ironwork. Nobody had time to remove the bodies, and for days, they hung there.

'The two companies had a busy and rather uncomfortable night, sweeping in so many prisoners that they did not know what to do with them. At first, they crammed the Germans into the little chambers in the side of the bridge, but these soon overflowed, and the prisoners complained bitterly about bad housing conditions. No 4 Company appealed for help. "We have three hundred prisoners, and more are coming in".'

In making a plan for the advance to the Rhine, the Guards had very little intelligence to work with. The historian continues:

'The Americans, who were actually in contact with the Germans to the north and east, could not give much information either, except that the Germans seemed to be well established around Elst, a town half way to Arnhem. A deserter from these Germans said that they had been ordered not to attack but dig-in and hold the road. The best information came from a captured map. The railway line to Arnhem runs parallel to the road a mile to the right-hand side. Halfway to Elst is Bessen station, connected with the main road by a low thickly hedged lane. On the map the station and lane were covered with German conventional signs for anti-tank guns and the whole area was dotted with infantry positions.'

As was feared, a strong German blocking position was already in place and was being reinforced by SS *Brigadeführer* Heinz Harmel's 10th *Frundsburg* SS Panzer Division. No less than sixteen tanks had been ferried across to the Island, a few of which had been used in Nijmegen. Also across the Rhine, were the equivalent of a battalion and a half of 22 SS Panzer Grenadier Regiment and a weak battalion of reservist infantry belonging to *Kampfgruppe* Hartung. Remnants of the *Hoenstaufen*'s Recce Battalion were also in position blocking the road at Elst. Available to give fire support were SS *Hauptsturmführer* Schwappacher's 21 Battery of SS Artillery Training and Replacement Regiment 5, who were well established in positions in the village of Oosterhout. Throughout the night, efforts to get additional SS infantry and tanks across the Rhine onto the Island, via an improvised ferry at Pannerden, were doubled. A hasty counter-attack against the Bemmel sector, the following morning failed to penetrate the now properly co-ordinated defences of the US Parachute Infantry Regiment (504 PIR).

Despite the growing evidence of the enemy strength, the Irish Guards' attack was nonetheless, to be directed along the main road to Arnhem, as the 1st Airborne Division's situation was now known to be

Tanks of the Irish Guards crossing on to the Island on the morning of 21 September.

desperate. Optimistically, the Guards were told that it was assessed 'the opposition would be slight and would anyway be disorganized by the Polish Parachute Brigade, who were to be dropped round Elst that afternoon'. Having been relieved of their task of guarding the Grave Bridge by 4 Dorset, the Welsh Guards Group was to join the later stages of the attack. To support the Irish Guards' attack:

> *'Colonel JOE Vandeleur demanded all available artillery and Typhoon support. This did not amount to very much. The advance to Nijmegen had been so rapid that the majority of the guns had not yet caught up and there was no large reserve of ammunition... Colonel Joe had to be content with a call on a limited number of Typhoons and the support of only one of the Division's field [artillery] regiments, as the other one had gone south with the Coldstream Group to protect the supply route.'*

Battle preparations, orders and regrouping took all morning to complete. Meanwhile, the Germans continued to strengthen their positions. An extract from a situation report to XXX Corps from their recce regiment, 2nd Household Cavalry Regiment (2 HCR), passed on some disturbing information at 1015 hours; 'Enemy appear to be holding ELST 7171 fairly strongly. Approx 20 tks reported

'Joe' Vandeleur

25

View from the turret of Kampfgruppe Knaust's leading panzer Mk III as it crosses the Arnhem Bridge onto the Island.

moving SOUTH in this area'. After three days of fighting at the Arnhem Bridge, the wreckage of battle was cleared on the morning of 21 September and *Kampfgruppe* Knaust was now arriving at the German *Schwerepunkt* on the Island. With 1st Airborne Division confined to a shrinking perimeter, of little operational significance, four miles to the west at Oosterbeek, the Germans were able to concentrate troops on the Island.

Kampfgruppe Knaust was an *ad hoc* unit, consisting of a seasoned battalion of *Wehrmacht* infantry volunteers and a mixed bag of at least eight armoured vehicles, including Tigers, Panthers, Mark IV *Sturmgushutze* and obsolescent Mark IIIs. It is a measure of the loss of air superiority, which the Allies had enjoyed since D-Day, that the Germans were able to move in daylight without being attacked by fighter-bombers. Allied airspace control measures, designed to deconflict strike and transport aircraft, were ponderous and the early autumn weather was becoming unpredictable for UK and continental based air operations.

The artillery barrage that preceded the Irish Guards' attack concentrated on positions taken from the captured enemy map. Not only was this fire 'map predicted' and, therefore, slightly speculative but it was also much lighter than the Guards had become used to. While the artillery was firing, the forty-seven tanks of 2 Irish Guards formed up on the road through Lent, with its leading troop, commanded by Lieutenant Samuelson, under the railway bridge that

Sergeant Robinson had reached the evening before. Number 1 Squadron was to lead, followed by Number 2 Company, mounted on the Shermans of Number 2 Squadron. Following behind were 3 Squadron and the remainder of the infantry of 3 Irish Guards.

H-Hour was at 1330 hours.

'For ten minutes and two miles all went well, though the column was driving along an open road raised six feet above the surrounding countryside. The leading column reached a solitary farm surrounded by an orchard, which was an island in the bare open ground stretching south from the suspected enemy positions. They could see in front of them a line of trees at right angles to the main road. Behind those trees ran the side road to Bessen. That was where the captured map marked the enemy guns. The map was right.'

However, a German *Sturmguschutz* opened fire down the road, as the leading troop came into the open and quickly knocked out three Shermans. Further back in the column, *Spandau* fire forced the infantrymen of Major Hendry Number 2 Company to 'dive straight off the tanks into the ditches on either side'. The advance halted behind the knocked out tanks, with no way off the road flanked by ditches. The seven guns in the hedge subsequently proved to be old French 75mm pieces, without armour piercing ammunition. This was just as well for the Irish Guards, as their tanks and soft-skin vehicles were sitting targets, silhouetted on the elevated roadway. Colonel Giles Vandeleur came forward to the head of the column braving,

'German infantry in the ditches with Spandaus *and "squeeze guns" kept firing down the middle and sides of the road – very noisy and uncomfortable'.*

A Sturmgeshütz 40 Ausf G, assault gun, with Schürzen (armoured skirts).

The view looking north and north-east from point X on map below.

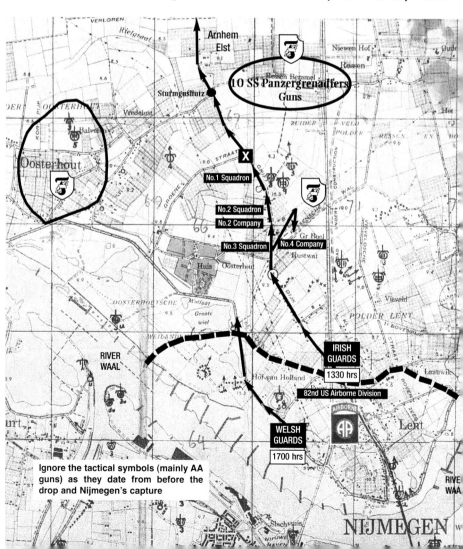

Ignore the tactical symbols (mainly AA guns) as they date from before the drop and Nijmegen's capture

With enemy armour to his front, guns to the flanks and only a few of his tanks able to engage the enemy without fatally exposing themselves to the *Sturmguschutz*, infantry were needed. Going back down the column, Colonel Giles Vandeleur agreed with his cousin Colonel Joe that fire support was also required if the Regiment was to break out from the road through the orchards, across the open ground to Elst.

At this point, the fire support arrangements failed. A few Typhoons were waiting in a 'Cab Rank' but 'the RAF control set broke down and then a second set was sent forward, which also broke down, so there was no communication with aircraft'. According to the MARKET GARDEN report, 'The tanks lacked vital support at a critical moment of the battle'. In short, there was to be no overwhelming air attack that had enabled the Irish Guards to break out of the Neerpelt Bridgehead, in similar circumstances, on the first day of the MARKET GARDEN. To make matters worse, the normally slick artillery support procedures also failed. The regimental historian described the Irishmen's reaction to this unfamiliar situation:

> 'The Group was at first disappointed and then very angry that no sound came from their guns. It was an hour before the first shells landed, but it was difficult to observe effects. The 3-inch mortar platoon, however, opened fire inside ten minutes.'

In reply, the Germans engaged the Guards stuck on the roads and in the ditches, with an increasing volume of artillery and mortar fire, including *Nebelwerfers* or as the British knew them 'Moaning Minnies'. One of the fearsome 320mm rocket propelled projectiles, pitched into the roadside ditch killing fifteen Guardsmen.

At 1530 hours, Major Hazlewood (No. 4 Company), tasked to

An SS soldier using an obsolescent, but still effective, MG34.

deliver the attack on the German positions on the railway line, arrived ahead of his company to prepare his battle orders. However, it was immediately apparent to him that the enemy *Spandaus* had not been suppressed but were dominating the four hundred yards of open no man's land.

'He reported to Colonel Joe that if the attack were to succeed, he would need the tanks supporting on the road and guns pouring shells into the German position.' No further support was available from the artillery and exposing the tanks would have led to their certain destruction by the Sturmguschutze. The Brigade Commander, Brigadier Gawtkin agreed to 'Major Hazlewood being ordered to take his company and No. 3 Squadron and try to work around the right flank by the railway line.'

Number 4 Company Irish Guards, supported by Shermans, cleared the orchards towards the railway line. However,

'as soon as they debouched on the open ground, the tanks were accurately engaged and the infantry pinned down by machine gun fire. It was an impasse. The attack never got under way.'

The Guards described the ammunition starved fire support as 'feeble shelling of the enemy position that did nothing to loosen the situation'. The problem was that, in the close country 'The anti-tank guns could not be pinpointed, as anyone who went forward immediately came under heavy fire'.

Major Orde of the Household Cavalry Regiment was watching this attack, which accidentally coincided with the much delayed drop of the Polish Airborne Brigade (see Chapter 3). He recorded:

'The ground battle, which had appeared to halt momentarily to gaze skyward at the arriving Poles, was quickly jerked back to its own sphere of action by a thud, followed by the crackle of exploding bullets, as yet another Irish Guards tank was hit and burst into flames. Traffic piled up behind the stricken Sherman and although other tanks tried every trick they knew to get off the road and continue across country, they only succeeded in getting themselves hopelessly bogged down.'

A radio message logged at 1800 hours, in XXX Corps's war diary from Guards Armoured Division recorded that:

'IG Gp now fully deployed. Inf Bn have had quite a number of cas. WG group trying to get round left but not making much progress. Inf

Irish Guardsmen advancing through the orchards while under fire.

As indicated in the SITREP above, the Welsh Guards Group were in action on the left flank in similar circumstances. However, it had already been a long and frustrating day for the Welshmen. Sitting in his Cromwell's turret, Major Fisher of No. 1 Squadron jotted down his impressions, while ahead of them the road to Arnhem was blocked:

'1.0 p.m.   My tank is just crossing the Waal.

1.15 p.m. We are stationary on the bridge ... it is slightly uncomfortable as we are a perfect, silhouetted target for German bombers, if any.

2 p.m. This bridge is not attractive ... There is a certain amount of small-arms fire from time to time, but I can't make out quite where from.

2.15 p.m.   When I was out of my tank just now a bullet whistled past my nose – literally. Soon after we had a mortar concentration all round us ... now there are lots of enemy planes over us. One man has

Welsh Guards' Cromwells crossing the Nijmegen Bridge on the afternoon of 21st September watched by troopers of US 505 PIR.

Pen & Sword Books
FREEPOST SF5
47 Church Street
BARNSLEY
South Yorkshire
S70 2BR

DISCOVER MORE ABOUT HISTORY ✂

Pen & Sword Books now offer over 3,000 titles in print covering all aspects of history including Military, Maritime, Aviation, Local, Family, Transport, Crime, Political and soon Social History. We also do books on nostalgia and have now introduced a range of military DVD's and Historical Fiction. If you would like to receive our catalogues and leaflets on new books and offers, please fill in the details below and return this card [no postage required].

Alternatively, register online at www.pen-and-sword.co.uk.

[Please note: we do not sell data information to any third party companies].

Visit www.WarfareMagazine.co.uk for free military history content including commemorative anniversary articles, military news, reviews, competitions and new product releases.

Title .... Name..

Address...

.... Postcode............................

Email Address ....

If you wish to receive our email newsletter, please tick here

Website: www.pen-and-sword.co.uk • Email: enquiries@pen-and-sword.co.uk

Telephone: 01226 734222 • Fax: 01226 734438

*been slightly wounded in the squadron. What a bloody place to be
sitting!*

*2.45 p.m.   More planes over us quite low. This is an unpleasant
situation I shall not forget this bridge for a long time.*

*3.15 p.m.   More shelling and mortaring. Brigade, Division and
Corps Commanders have all gone forward in succession to make a plan
to deal with the opposition. Meanwhile we stay on this dammed bridge.'*

As a result of the senior officers going forward, the Welsh Guards were
committed to an attack on the left flank shortly after 1700 hours. The
Welsh Guards, the infantry of the 1st Battalion were mounted on 2nd
Battalion's Cromwells, with only, the three leading tanks of Number 1
Squadron being unencumbered by infantry. The attack was to be
mounted along the dyke road past Hof van Holland (held by American
paratroopers) towards Oosterhout. However, German anti-tank guns
soon halted the leading Cromwells but the Welshmen arrived in time
to assist the 82nd Airborne Division in beating of an armoured counter-
attack by the *Frundsburg*, knocking out three tanks in the process. As
offensive action, this left flanking attack, 'never got under way' in any
meaningful form and was called off by Divisional Headquarters, as the
light failed. There was to be little rest for the Welsh Guards Group over
night, as they were ordered to prepare a limited attack to the east of the
bridgehead for the following morning.

By the afternoon of 21 September, SS *Brigadeführer* Heinz Harmel's
10th SS Panzer Division had been able to fully co-ordinate its defences,
making expert use of the cover and open terrain to produce
interlocking fields of fire. With insufficient artillery and air support to
neutralize the German anti-tank and machine guns, there was little
chance of breaking through 'such strong defences'. Therefore, with
daylight failing, the Guards were given orders to suspend their attacks,
which were to be renewed by the 43rd Wessex Division the following
day.

Having suffered heavy infantry casualties, the Irish Guards Group
withdrew a thousand yards to a harbour area. Here 'Lieutenant Rupert
Mahaffey, sitting in a ditch, told Major Hazlewood with gloomy
satisfaction that, out of all the platoon commanders who had landed in
Normandy, he was the only survivor'. With the 1st Airborne Division
marooned at Oosterbeek morale was at a low ebb. Guardsmen
Fitzgerald explained that:

*'I'd never seen so many miserable people in my life and I was one of
them. I had seen Guardsmen in my platoon blown to pieces and others*

A knocked-out Sherman that was subsequently pushed off the elevated main road into the ditch.

lying wounded on the road – screaming. The Jerries shot at anyone who went forward to help. We were wet, cold, tired, had been beaten back and let down by the artillery.'

Commenting on the Allied plan, a post-war instructor at the Dutch Staff College said, that an attack up the road from Nijmegen to Arnhem was set every year for the Colonels' promotion exam.

'It was the sack for those who went straight up the road. If the officer decided to go left flanking, he got a brigade. The attack up the main road is not on – certainly not with tanks.'

CHAPTER THREE

FIRE SUPPORT AND THE POLISH PARACHUTE BRIGADE'S DROP

On 21 September, while the Irish Guards were attacking north, the main body of XXX Corps was moving up to Nijmegen; having been badly delayed by enemy action and traffic chaos. With XXX Corps were the medium guns of the Corps Artillery, which were now coming within range of Arnhem. Meanwhile, back in England, the weather was improving sufficiently to allow the final Allied airborne element to leave their airfields. As the morning mist cleared men of the much-delayed 1st Independent Polish Airborne Brigade were briefed on the latest snippets of information on the situation at Arnhem.

Contact with 1st Airborne Division and Fire Support

Most of 1st Airborne's radio sets only had a reliable range of just three miles. This was inadequate to cover the distance between Divisional Headquarters, at the Hartenstine, and the Arnhem Bridge eight miles away. The worst fears of the Divisional Signals had been realized. However, as the days since the drop went by, the beleaguered paratroopers thought that 'surely XXX Corps must be getting near'. On the morning of 21 September, 1st Airborne redoubled attempts to contact to them by radio. Royal Artillery signaller Sergeant Patten, working in 1st Airborne Light Battery's command post, climbed a small factory's chimney with an antenna for his 22 Set. Below him, Captain McMillan (1 Forward Observation Unit) started to tune his radio through the frequencies, until he came on the unmistakable traffic of a gunner radio net. However, without the correct radio authentication codes he was not welcome! Through good fortune, he had joined the net of 64 Medium Regiment RA, whose 4.5 and 5.5-inch guns were the only XXX Corps gunners capable of assisting 1st Airborne Division at that time. This is one of the few significant pieces of good fortune in an operation that seemed dogged by ill luck from start to finish.

At 0935 hours, 64 Medium's Second in Command was in the regimental command post:

> *'Suddenly the smoothness of the net was broken by a station using an unknown call sign. He was asking permission to come in on our net. He was ordered off. He persisted. "We are being heavily shelled and*

mortared. Can you help us?" The voice was calm ... we asked who he
was. "The people that you are trying to join up with" the voice replied.
It seemed incredible, but it must, it could only be, 1st Airborne.'

Even if the Second in Command, Major Sam Allridge, was convinced, other officers and radio operators were suspicious of an unauthenticated station joining their net. At 1030 hours, XXX Corps's Commander Corps Royal Artillery (CCRA) alerted General Horrocks's HQ about the new contact. The watchkeeper recorded: 'Intercept from 1 Airborne Div asking for fire on 703777. This situation is being challenged and reference checked and G (Ops) being informed of result.' As the Airborne Gunners did not have XXX Corps codes, another 'reference' had to be found. In the relatively small British Army, with a tight regimental system, names were an obvious choice. The CCRA's first question was to verify the surname of the voice from Arnhem, and the reply came, 'Yes, and my Christian name is Robert'. The next question was the name of a mutual acquaintance in the Royal Artillery, 'Armitage, Charles Armitage' were the words that convinced. To those still sceptical in 64 Medium's command post, Major Allridge ordered, 'Not so much bloody argument, get into action!' Artillery Headquarters, 1st Airborne Division armed with 64 Medium's frequency tuned their high power No. 19 Set and joined their net. The British Paratroopers now had a lifeline that was to preserve the Perimeter over the following four days.

A 4.5-inch gun of 64 Medium Regiment in action on the outskirts of Nijmegen. Note the power station chimney.

At 1035 hours, 211 Battery reported 'Ready for action'. They had been passed three targets by 1st Airborne. Two were out of range but the third, with their 4.5-inch guns firing Super Charge, could just be engaged. The Gunners made two corrections to a single gun's fall of shot and then the lone gun 'fired for effect' at rate 3 (three rounds per minute), as a confidence builder. Many paratroopers have recalled the arrival of the shells on the perimeter. Typical of the recollections is that of a Corporal from the South Staffords:

'I remember the first time that XXX Corps Artillery fired in support of us. We could hear something big coming from an unusual direction – south – was it ours or theirs? Anyhow, we didn't wait to find out but got our heads down. The shells crashed into the enemy lines. They were ours! I can't tell you how pleased we were when we realised that XXX Corps was getting close.'

More guns opened fire and soon the whole battery was in action.

At 1200 hours, 211 Battery's troops started to leapfrog forward 4,000 yards, retaining half the Battery's guns in action at any one time. By moving the guns forward to the area of the power station in Nijmegen, 64 Medium could support the whole of the Perimeter. Meanwhile, in Oosterbeek, the antenna was moved to the Hemelse Berg Park Hillock near the Hartenstine where the 1st Airborne's Artillery Brigade Major took control of the vital link. During the afternoon, 64 Medium's 5.5-inch gun batteries came into range and then, at 1600 hours, the 155mm guns of 419 Heavy Battery, which were attached from 5th Army Group Royal Artillery (5 AGRA), were in action. The Germans, seemingly stunned by this new development, reduced their attacks and, during the night, 64 Medium were only called to fire two defensive fire tasks; one at midnight and the second at 0540 hours – just before dawn.

The following day (22 September), 64 Medium engaged thirty-one targets around the Perimeter and fired a fire plan that covered a minor operation to stabilize the Airborne Division's positions and on 23 September they fired twenty-three fire-missions. With only the Number 19 HP set anything like reliable, as Captain Lewis Golden of 1st Airborne Signals described:

'Artillery officers out with battalions would call for fire by any

An airborne artillery radio operator.

37

means available to them. They were very resourceful. Often those calls had to be transmitted over a series of radio networks, ending with the well disciplined [radio] *net of 64th Medium Regiment group. But there were no mistakes; and the absence of any margin of error had no greater consequence than a period of intense anxiety for the controlling officers... The only reliable links established were those to 64th Medium Regiment, and therefore they had to carry an immense weight of traffic. Even that network was not free of problems at night, notwithstanding the boost given by a radio relay station sent out in the direction of Arnhem with the advanced headquarters of the Irish Guards battalion* [in the area north of Lent].'

Lieutenant Douglas Goddard

In recognition of the highly significant part played in ensuring their survival, 1st Airborne Division presented each gunner of 64 Medium Regiment a small Pegasus badge, which was authorised to be worn on the lower sleeve of their battledress. From 21 September onwards, the majority of XXX Corps's scarce artillery ammunition was used to support the paratroopers in the Oosterbeek Perimeter.

Over the following days, adding weight to the artillery support available to 1st Airborne were the seventy-two 25-pounders of 43rd Wessex Division, whose field batteries were coming into range. Amongst the Wessex gunners, was Lieutenant Douglas Goddard, the Gun Position Officer 220 Battery, 112 Field Regiment RA, who recalls some of the difficulties:

'*On the 23rd we crossed the Nijmegen Bridge to come into action in the area of Oosterhout, which put us within range of the 1st Airborne's pocket and enabled us to reinforce 64 Medium and 419 Heavy Battery with artillery support... 1st Airborne's fire orders were transmitted via 64 Medium's radio net which was now the CRA's net as well.*

'*The area around Oosterhout that we are occupying has no infantry protection since infantry moved up and we were under sniper and shellfire from German positions towards Elst. When we occupied a gun position I was normally given an optimum arc of 30 degrees that I was expected to cover but in this case the highly unusual order "Arc 270 degrees" was given. We suffered casualties from enemy fire while we were attempting to concentrate on responding to calls for fire from all directions – 129 Brigade on the right, 214 on the left and the Poles and*

1st Airborne centre. Despite the prudent decision to keep 'A' Echelon ammunition lorries with us and that we therefore had some 350 rounds per gun at the outset, we were getting worryingly short of ammunition, with the number of calls for fire growing rapidly. With the Lines of Communication cut behind us no ammunition or food was getting through. So we lived on the captured, unpalatable, German rations.

Sergeant George Upshall of 224 Battery, 94 Field Regiment RA described the conditions in which the gunners laboured:

'Having crossed the river onto the Island, the weather took a real hand in events and this was the start of the worst fortnight of the war for me. It just rained and rained... The roads were narrow and you couldn't get off them to pass anything, so we had problems with the rear guard of the tanks and all the time there was a risk of snipers. We soon found ourselves in action and digging pits. The ground was quite easy to dig but the trouble was the rain turned everything into mud. As well as being wet, we were covered in mud up to our knees and it became very tiring to work day and night like that, in addition to the fact that we were being continually shelled. On the first night, our ammunition group managed to get through and we took several tons of shells for each gun. It was becoming a desperate fight and the guns were not silent for long at any time. We were unable to lie down anywhere because of the mud and water, so we would cat-nap sitting on an ammo box or on the trail of the gun! In my case, I found myself standing with one hand on the trail handspike and suddenly becoming conscious of the tannoy calling "Take post – Troop target."... the voice of the Gun Position Officer brought everyone to life at once with a clear head and mind.

'At one time I had only 3 HE shells, 6 chemical and 2 AP shot left – all my smoke shells were gone. Things were looking grim.'

The Drop of the Polish Parachute Brigade

Just as SS-*Brigadeführer* Harmel's SS *Frundsberg Kampgruppe* was beginning to confidently report that they were able to hold the renewed Allied attack on the road to Arnhem, more paratroopers dropped behind them. This event brought a whole new set of potentially dangerous threats for the Germans to deal with. However, now having control of the Arnhem Bridge, II SS Panzer *Korps* was well positioned to respond quickly.

The 1st Independent Polish Parachute Brigade was formed in the autumn of 1941, by Brigadier Stanislaw Sosabowski under the auspices of the Polish Government in exile. Soldiers were recruited from Poles who had escaped from the German occupation and found their way

Repeatedly delayed due to weather, Polish paratroopers await the order to emplane.

Britain. Sosabowski, or as he was know by his soldiers, 'Sosab', raised the Brigade with 'independent' status. That is to say, it had its own organic artillery, engineers, supply system, signals, medical units, etc. The Brigade's airborne element numbered 1,690 men with a sea tail of 532 men. In recognition of his considerable experience of war, both practical and theoretical (he had commanded the Polish War College) Sosabowski was promoted to Major General in early September 1944. This promotion was to have a serious effect on relationships with other commanders during the coming battle.

In June 1944, the Brigade was placed under command of SHAEF. However, later the same month, when the Allied Airborne Army formed, the Polish paratroopers retained their 'independent' status but, as Operation COMET grew into MARKET GARDEN, the Poles were attached to 1st Airborne Division for the Arnhem battle.

The original plan had been to drop the Poles on Tuesday 19 September, however, bad weather prevented the Brigade's parachute element from taking off and only the gliders had landed on their LZ to the north-west of the Arnhem. The Germans were expecting them and the Brigade's support element was destroyed. The three Polish parachute battalions were to have landed at DZ K, immediately south of the Arnhem Bridge. From here, the plan was that they were to take over defence of the Bridge from 1 Para Brigade, which would allow the British paratroopers to expand the bridgehead north of the Rhine. However, by 21 September it was clear that 2 PARA's tenuous hold on the northern end of the Arnhem Bridge had been lost and the plan need changing. The Poles would still have to drop south of the Rhine and cross via the Driel

Major General Sosabowski

Ferry into the Perimeter. The first indication received by XXX Corps that plans for the Poles' drop had changed, was in a message passed from the co-located Airborne Corps HQ, at 1520 hours while the Irish Guards were attempting to drive north:

'1 AB Div requests Polish Para Bde land DZ 685754 – 698775 – 690130 – 682737 NOT DZ K. Poles to cross by ferry 686767 and conc area HEMELSCH BERG 6977.'

By 1400 hours, the weather had cleared over England and 114 Dakotas carrying the Poles took off. However, over the Continent weather conditions were marginal for parachute operations, with low scudding cloud. Forty-one aircraft, containing mostly 1st Polish Parachute Battalion, turned back and returned to their bases, while three aircraft diverted to Brussels. Worse, over the battle area, the *Luftwaffe* had gained air superiority and a hundred enemy fighters of *Jagdgeschhwaders* 2, 11 and 26, forewarned by coastal flak batteries, were waiting for the Dakotas. In the ensuing dogfight with Allied fighter escorts, twenty-five German aircraft broke through the screen and shot down thirteen of the slow transports. Anti-aircraft fire from the Island and nearby Arnhem inflicted further losses. The formation of the remaining Dakota aircraft could not manoeuvre and, consequently, they had a single chance to identify the DZ through breaks in the cloud and drop their stick of paratroopers.

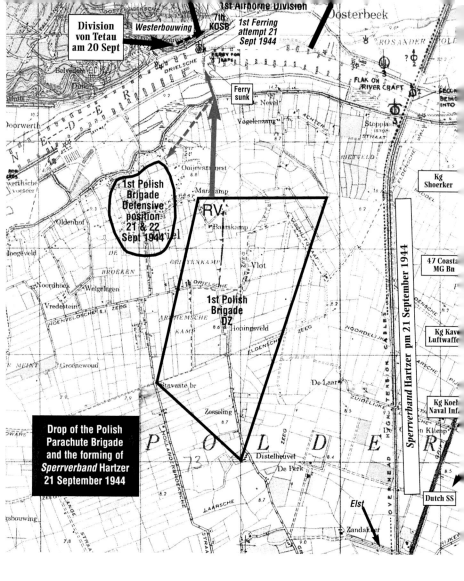

The number of Poles that actually jumped at 1715 hours, from fifty-three aircraft, is thought to have been between 750 and 950 men, with Major General Sosabowski and his headquarters amongst them. As the Polish paratroopers dropped, laden with as much ammunition as their parachutes would bear, they came under machine gun fire, which caused a number of casualties. Opposition in the area of the DZ was swept aside as the Poles headed for the Rhine and the Driel – Heveadorp Ferry. To Sosabowski's consternation, the ferry was lying on its side, half submerged, having been scuttled, only shortly before, by the ferryman who feared that the Germans may have used it. To make matters worse, the Poles standing forlornly on the riverbank, came under machine gun fire from the Arnhem side. Earlier that very day, the Worrowski Battalion of the Herman Göring Regiment had driven a platoon of B Company 7 KOSB off the Westerbouwing Heights opposite the ferry. In the confused fighting that had forced General Urquhart to form the Perimeter, on ground not of his choosing, the tactical importance of the Westerbouwing Heights had been missed. However, it is fair to say that neither side had fully appreciated the value of the position until the Germans stumbled on the lightly defended bluff. The loss of the Westerbouwing Heights was to be a serious disadvantage to Allied attempts to cross the Rhine. Not only were the Germans now in possession of a position that dominated the river, one hundred feet below, but they also overlooked much of the Island. Unable to cross the river, General Sosabowski took his brigade to nearby Driel and established defensive positions. Lacking heavy support weapons, the Poles were in a dangerously exposed position.

Across the river, there were two contrasting reactions to the arrival of the Poles. First, General Urquhart:

> 'At 5.15 p.m. came the encouraging news that the Poles were arriving on their dropping zone south of the river just east of Driel. From the southern part of our perimeter, the spire of Driel Church was a solitary and prominent landmark in the flat land beyond the river. By now, however, the Heveadrop Ferry by which we might have got the

A pre-war view from Westerbouwing overlooking the area of the Island used by the Poles as a DZ and the Driel-Heveadorp Ferry.

Polish paras at Driel.

Poles across had fallen into German hands and my chief engineer Eddie Myers was having little luck in gathering the boats and rafts necessary to ferry the Poles. He planned to use Jeep trailers for the purpose and now dispatched one of his field squadrons to see what it could do.'

However, the Germans were far from 'encouraged'. They were exhausted having, after a bitter battle, recaptured the Arnhem Bridge and had started to attack the Perimeter with every expectation of success. The Germans had been content that, while they had lost the Nijmegen crossings, 10 SS Panzer Division was containing the over

The ruins of the café on the high ground at Westerbouwing. Once the Germans had captured this position they could observe troop movements across much of the Island opposite.

extended XXX Corps. Nonetheless, their reaction to the new airborne threat was, typically, both swift and positive. *Kampfguppe* Knaust were already moving to reinforce 10 SS Panzer Division and was ordered by II SS Panzer *Korps* 'to employ the leading elements of the newly arrived Battalion "Knaust" in Elst against this new threat without delay'. A part of Knaust's command duly attacked west through Elst but their advance quickly lost momentum as the tanks tried to feel their way through the ditches and dykes that drained polder land beyond the village. The Germans withdrew and started to prepare defensive positions around Elst. The German's main reaction to the arrival of the Poles was to form a *Sperrverband* (barrier position) along the embankment of the Arnhem – Nijmegen railway line. No less than 2,500 troops, in five battalions were quickly deployed. Three battalions, one of which was armed with medium machine guns, comprised naval personnel or marines who had been manning North Sea coastal positions and had originally been directed to Oosterbeek. Of the other two battalions, one was *Luftwaffe* and the other was made up of Dutch SS troops. Over the following days, this force was strengthened with armour and artillery. The creation of the *Sperrverband* under SS-*Obersturmbannführer* Hartzer, is yet another example of the German

SS-Obersturmbannführer Hartzer

Captured German soldiers held in a pig pen at Driel are watched over by their Polish captors.

genius for improvising an effective defence.

21 September had opened with considerable promise for the Allies but had ended with very little progress having been made. At the end of a tenuous link stretching back sixty miles to the Belgian border, XXX Corps had been in action not only on the Island but also in their rear on the Groesbeek Heights and on Hell's Highway.

The drop of the Polish Brigade was, in the uncertainty of battle, perceived by the Germans to be a highly significant threat. However, with the weather limiting the number of men dropped, the ferry being scuttled and Westerbouwing in German hands, the speedy German reaction effectively neutralised the Poles. But, it can be argued that formation of *Sperrverband* Hartzer drew vital Germans resources away from the battle to reduce the Perimeter and thus helped, along with the artillery, to prolong its existence. However, the drop also prompted the Germans to take the one action that would finally prevent XXX Corps's timely arrival on the Rhine: a significant reinforcement of the Island.

CHAPTER FOUR

OOSTERHOUT AND THE DASH TO DRIEL

43rd Wessex Division on Hell's Highway

Allied terrain analysis warned that, off the main road, the Island was unsuitable for armoured operations and, that with strong German resistance, an infantry division was needed to lead the last ten miles to Arnhem. The 43rd Wessex Division had been waiting for three days in assembly areas on the heath land fifty miles to the south. Anticipating the capture of the Nijmegen Bridges, Lieutenant General Horrocks ordered Major General Thomas to be prepared to move early on 20 September.

The 43rd, however, found that covering the fifty miles up Hell's Highway from the Corps Rear Area to the front at Nijmegen, was painfully slow. Convoy commanders argued for priority with other troops who were moving to repel German counter-attacks and, exasperated military policemen attempted to gain some semblance of order according to constantly changing priorities. Signalman Stan Proctor, a Royal Signals operator with Headquarters 214 Brigade:

'...was on listening watch in the command vehicle when a voice in my earphones said: "Jig York Mike – Sunray Major here [a superior commander]. *Message for Sunray Minor* [a more junior commander], *over." It was the Divisional Commander; General Thomas and he wanted our Brigadier* [Essame]. *The Brigadier picked up his microphone "Jig York Mike, Sunray Minor here, over" "Jig York Mike, Sunray Major to Sunray Minor – Uncurl – over." "Jig York Mike – Sunray Minor to Sunray Major – bugger off – out!" I marvelled at this – what would happen to the Brigadier? Presumably, he knew what he was doing and there was no practical prospect of the Brigade "uncurling" – or getting onto the road. I learned that the General was quick to dismiss officers who displeased him but*

Signalman Stan Proctor.

Infantry of 7 Somerset LI mounted in Bren-gun carriers and Dukws waiting on Hell's Highway, morning 20 September.

also that our Brigadier was one of the few who stood up to him and got away with it.'

When the Wessex eventually got onto the road, their divisional column, of 3,300 vehicles, came to an abrupt halt. Ahead, 107 Panzer Brigade's dawn attack on the Son Bridge, held by 101st Airborne Division, had blocked Hell's Highway. Halted for five hours, the Division was on the move again by mid-day. Led by the armoured cars of 43rd Recce Regiment, the Division's order of march was 130 Brigade, 214 Brigade, the Netherlands Brigade (under command) and 129 Brigade, followed by only the most vital supply vehicles. The bulk of the Division's logistic vehicles were left south of the Escaut Canal. The infantry rode in the large amphibious Dukws that proved to be unsuitable for use on narrow roads in heavy traffic. Lieutenant Colonel George Taylor of 5 Duke of Cornwall's Light Infantry recalled how:

'As we moved up the road we realised what a magnificent job General Maxwell Taylor's, 101st Airborne Division had done, securing five of the six bridges over rivers and canals. The sixth bridge, the enemy were able to blow up in their faces.'

129 Brigade were near Eindhoven when 101st Airborne requested 94 Field Regiment RA to engage Germans on the road to their front. Sergeant George Upshall of 224 Battery recalls that:

'We were showered with flowers and fruit and as the column slowed down in the outskirts of a town, some youngsters jumped onto the gun and trailer.

'At one time I had six boys riding on my gun when our dispatch Rider rode back along the line to tell us that we would be coming into action about a mile up the road. We knew this would mean speeding up

and a rough ride for the guns bouncing over the ground... I jumped off the tractor and began to pull the boys off while the gun was still moving, but the people had other ideas and I was soon overcome with shaking hands... My No. 3 saw what was happening and told our driver to keep going slowly. I eventually cleared everyone off the gun and jumped onto the tractor as we increased speed. Almost at once the signal for "Crash Action" was passed back along the line and we saw the leading tractor turn into a field on the left of the road and within three minutes, the guns were in action with the "Zero Line" recorded by compass. After firing five rounds per gun, we were told that the enemy had counter-attacked the [American] airborne troops holding the next bridge and the [British] tanks had called for support. The next order was to "dig-in".'

Still on the road, approaching Grave, during the night of 20/21 September, were 112 Field Regiment RA, who, along with the rest of the Division, were ignoring the Corps order not to move after dark. Lieutenant Douglas Goddard, gun-position officer of 220 Battery, recalls an incident all too common in slow moving convoys:

'I was leading the Battery column. Sometime after dark, we were halted on the road for some unknown reason and having been standing up in the commanders hatch in the truck I dozed off and so must my driver. Anyway, I suddenly woke to find that the column was no longer in front of me and I had 2/3rds of the Division behind me – there must have been over 3,000 vehicles behind me! We drove on stealthily and caught up with the column, which had fortunately for me, been held up again. Thank goodness only my driver knew of this at the time and it did not seem to affect the conduct of the operation too much. In mitigation, it should be said that we had had hardly any sleep for the previous three days.'

Also in the column were 4 Wiltshire. Their historian recalled a similar incident that broke the battalion's column:

'...a minor breakdown at the end of B Company caused the rear portion of the column to halt. Major Robbins, commanding C Company, who were following, was asked for the route... it was a very difficult question to answer: precious minutes went by... Maj Robbins eventually decided on which road he thought was the right one and pushed on. Enemy tanks could be heard plainly, with much shooting...

'As the tanks seemed to draw still nearer, Major Robbins ordered lights to be switched on in a desperate effort to increase speed. He sent a despatch rider from the Carrier

Major Robbins MC

The Wiltshires of 129 Brigade dug-in on the western outskirts of Nijmegen, PM 21 September 1944.

Platoon to try to catch up with the remainder of the column: no results were achieved on the deserted roads. By what seemed sheer luck the column caught up with the rest of the Battalion at Grave, two hours late. One wrong turning could have led the whole Brigade Group into the 'bag'; it appeared later that [129] Brigade Headquarters and the other two battalions following behind had been unaware of what had been happening.'

During the course of 20 September, General Thomas went ahead to meet General Horrocks at Corps Tactical Headquarters, south of Nijmegen. In order to enable the Welsh Guards to rejoin the remainder of the increasingly hard-pressed Guards Armoured Division, 4 Dorset were to take over guarding the vital Waal Bridge at Grave. Three companies of Dorset Territorial Army soldiers were to hold the Bridge, while a fourth company moved to defend the Neerbosch Bridge on the Maas-Waal Canal. Other instructions given to General Thomas were that 43rd Recce Regiment along with 12 Kings Royal Rifle Corps, in their half-tracks, were to form a screen between the Maas and the Waal west of Nijmegen. The remainder of 130 Brigade was to clear Nijmegen in detail the following morning.

Later that evening (20 September), with only the leading elements of 43 Wessex Division concentrating to the south-west of Nijmegen, 214 Brigade's senior commanders moved to the bank of the Waal. They were to spearhead the next attempt to reach Arnhem. Accompanying them was Lieutenant Colonel George Taylor, who recalls a meeting:

'I went ahead to carry out a recce from the Bridge with the Brigadier and the COs of the Brigade. They left me on the Bridge and it was here

that I met General Horrocks, as usual well forward seeing things for himself. He told me that the enemy were beginning to recover their balance and was stubbornly holding a line north of the bridge and preventing the Guards breaking through to reach the hard pressed British Airborne Division at Arnhem... Horrocks said, "What would you do George?" I said, "Do a left hook and use Dukws to cross behind the enemy holding Oosterhout". I did not believe that they had much depth behind the village. This proved to be so.'

This suggestion reflected the plan that was already forming in the minds of Generals Horrocks and Thomas, and had already been attempted late that day by the tanks of the Welsh Guards. However, as infantry, the Wessex Division were not tied to the dangerously exposed roads across the Island.

Nijmegen and the Bridges

The Bridges had been taken but only a part of the city had been cleared and the enemy was still active. However, much of the German activity reported by the Dutch during the night of 20/21 September, was probably isolated groups making their way east to the safety of the German boarder. The following morning, while the Irish Guards were assembling for their attack, 43rd Wessex Division entered Nijmegen. Private O'Connell wrote; 'In one part of the town, it was all love, kisses, fruit and flowers: in the other, there was a barrage of bullets and shells'. However, with the methodical clearance by 5 Dorset and 7 Hampshire, opposition melted away. Major Hartwell of 5 Dorset recorded:

'This was quite the most fantastic operation; far from finding any Germans lurking in the town, it was with the greatest difficulty that any progress could be made through the excited occupants who festooned the troops with flowers and filled their pockets with apples.'

Signalman Stan Proctor, now forward with 1 Worcester's Signal Platoon, was on the riverbank in Nijmegen did, however, witness some action as he:

'...watched the air battle. Two Focke Wolfs dive down. We were shot up by American Thunderbolts that followed. One of these chased a Focke Wolf up the street beside us almost at lamppost height. The bullets from the Thunderbolt's machine guns sprayed the road as the Focke Wolf weaved among the buildings.'

Despite dealing with isolated German resistance, shelling and understandably exuberant Dutch people, by early afternoon, 5 Dorset crossed to the northern bank of the Waal, joining 505 US PIR around the two bridges. Meanwhile, 7 Hampshire took over defences of the Road

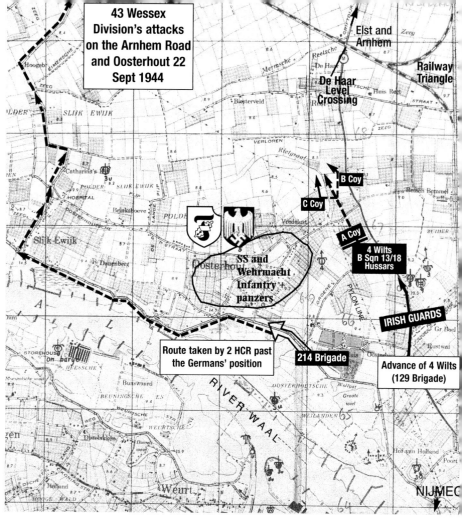

Route taken by 2 HCR past the Germans' position

and Rail Bridges on the Nijmegen bank.

The plan had been for the leading battlegroup of 214 Brigade, who were following the Dorsets and Hampshires, to cross the river into the Island bridgehead on the afternoon of 21 September. However, the slowness of 130 Brigade's clearance and continuing confusion in Nijmegen, combined with a lack of adequate maps, created further delays. Major Ivor Reeves of 7 Somerset LI, found conditions almost insurmountable in Nijmegen:

> 'The difficulty of collecting one's Order Group, of thinking and giving orders, of making oneself heard and linking the various sub units of supporting arms together – amongst the mass of the populace still crowded round, still cheering was impossible.'

In the confusion, a part of 7 Som LI's column became separated and most of the battalion was directed to the Road Bridge rather than the Rail Bridge. The result was that the Quarter Master and his cooks prepared the Battalion's evening meal amongst the Welsh Guards in the front line on the Island and sent it back to the companies still stuck to the rear in Nijmegen!

Brigadier Essame outlined the Division's plan for 22 September:

'Overnight, 43rd Wessex Division completed its concentration near the bridges and carried out its battle preparations. The Division's plan was for 129 Brigade to take over attempts to attack down the line of the Arnhem Road, while 214 Brigade was to attack around the German's right flank. 214 Brigade's attack was the divisional Main Effort but while 129 Brigade may well have made progress towards Arnhem, their primary purpose was to ensure the enemy's attention remained focused on the highway rather than on his flanks. Meanwhile, the Germans, in response to the Independent Polish Brigade's drop at Driel, had continued to pour troops onto the Island to contain the new threat.'

To complete the moves planned for 22 September, 130 Brigade were to be relieved at the Grave and Nijmegen bridges by the Dutch Brigade and 69 Brigade respectively. 130 Brigade was then to become the divisional reserve. Early on 22 September General Horrocks, realizing the desperate situation in Arnhem, signalled General Urquhart that '43 Div [have been] ordered to take all risks to effect relief today and are directed on ferry. If situation warrant you should withdraw to or cross ferry'.

The Household Cavalry Reach the Rhine

On the evening of 21 September, Lieutenant Colonel Able Smith of 2 HCR received orders from XXX Corps. He remembered them well:

'They stated, "Intelligence believes that the enemy [in Oosterhout] will withdraw during the night. 43 Infantry Division will relieve the Guards during the night, and continue the advance the next day. One squadron of 2 HCR will advance to Arnhem, covering 43 Division at first light."

'On receipt of these orders, I immediately drove off to 43rd Division Headquarters, as the intelligence appreciation of the enemy seemed extraordinary. The enemy had fought [the Guards] most tenaciously all day, and if they could hold us a little longer, the airborne troops would be doomed.'

However, shortly after dawn, the armoured cars of 2 HCR were preparing to advance ahead of 214 Brigade, as the Wessex's own recce squadrons were deployed to the west of Nijmegen. The early autumn fog favoured the cars of C Squadron, with visibility being about fifty feet. The leading troop under the command of Captain Wrottesley slipped along the road passed Oosterhout. They had seen one or two surprised 'Krauts' cooking breakfast, but they were swallowed up in the mist before either side could do anything much about it. However, Trooper John Knight, driving the second armoured car, from his position low in the hull:

> *'counted three Mk III Panzers at the limit of visibility along the south-eastern edge of the village. They obviously didn't see us or we were gone before they could react. We got through without further incident but the Poles near Driel were, I suppose, understandably trigger-happy.'*

Having passed through the German positions, Captain Wrottesley motored on to link up with the Poles at Driel. OC C Squadron risked sending another troop via the same route before the fog lifted. Lieutenant Young recalled, 'Things were exceptionally quiet at this time. We passed several Mark IVs [sic], which we liked to presume at the time had been knocked out, but we later discovered proved to be very much alive!'

The two troops, having arrived at Driel, spent a busy day answering questions from HQ XXX Corps, who took the unusual step of joining the Squdron's radio net. Among the questions asked were, the state of the Driel – Heveadorp Ferry? 'Destroyed by the Ferryman' and conditions on the banks of the Rhine? 'Difficult to reach, being steep and muddy'. In addition, Lieutenant Young acted as an observer for 64

Poles greet the HCR and brief Captain Wrottesley on the situation in Driel.

Armoured cars of 2 HCR photographed during MARKET GARDEN.

Medium Regiment, whose guns also helped break-up German attacks on Driel. The presence of 'jockeying' armoured cars, despite the fact that they became critically short of ammunition, was a significant factor in deterring the Germans from pressing home their attacks on the Poles. Lieutenant Young recalls fighting with the isolated Poles:

'The main attack on Driel began shortly after eleven o'clock, and at this point I had difficulty with the Polish general, who was anxious that we should use our cars as tanks, as there was still enemy armour in the area. The Polish general was charming but quite fanatical, and if he had thought it the least possible would have asked us to fly our armoured cars into battle! This attack, which was a particularly vicious one, lasted with little intermission until dark, and the Polish Forces were extremely grateful for the added firepower of our two troops.'

7 Somerset LI's Attack on Oosterhout

On the morning of 22 September, 214 Brigade's left flanking advance was to be astride a single minor road on the top of a tall dyke. Joining the Somersets were the Shermans of A Squadron 4/7 Dragoon Guards (4/7 DG). Captain John Stirling recalls:

'We linked up with an infantry battalion and, in the early morning mist, drove over the vast length of the railway bridge – some six hundred yards long, which was strewn with the bodies of the Germans who had tried to hold it. Then we swung left along the dyke road running high above the north bank of the river. The road was skyline suicide; to the left the bank was very steep, to the right were woods.'

Also joining the Somersets, was a troop of towed 17-pounder anti-tank guns and the forward observation officers of 179 Regt RA, who in addition to their own towed guns, had in support, the self-propelled 25-pounders of 431 Battery, the Essex Yeomanry. Completing the battlegroup, were 8 Middlesex's MMGs and heavy mortars. However, this fire support group was not as impressive as it sounds, as it only had first line scales of ammunition, with no immediate prospect of re-supply. Out of the question, were the mind numbing barrages of Normandy, as the Wessex Division's supply vehicles were stuck at various points on Hell's Highway. In addition, air support was not available. Consequently, it was vital that 214 Brigade used the limited stocks of ammunition wisely.

The enemy in Oosterhout had had plenty of time to prepare and comprised of elements of *Kampfgruppe* Knaust. Their anti-tank positions on the northern edge of Oosterhout, interlocked with the arcs of fire those of tanks positioned on the Nijmegen to Arnhem road, 1,000 yards away. The Mark III Panzers, spotted by John Knight on the southern outskirts of Oosterhout, were survivors of the Mielke Panzer Training Company that had been dispatched from its regiment in Biedefeldt to join *Kampfgruppe* Knaust. Previously they had fought with 9th SS Panzer Division during the final stages of the battle for the Arnhem Bridge and crossed onto the Island on 21 September.

On the banks of the Waal, just east of Oosterhout, the mist cleared at 0800 hours, to reveal A Squadron 4/7 DG and D Company 7 Som LI. They were caught out in the open, in full view of the enemy, having just emerged from the wooded belt that surrounded Huis Oosterhout. They came under heavy and accurate fire from *Kampfgruppe* Knaust, at a range of seven hundred yards. Unfortunately, when the two HCR troops had earlier successfully passed Oosterhout, Major General Thomas considered it probable that the enemy had withdrawn and, in order to save time and precious artillery ammunition, he cancelled the fire plan. The German Mark IIIs may have been obsolescent but their machine guns pinned down the Somersets and their main armament halted the advance of A Squadron's Shermans, who confined to the elevated dyke road, made excellent targets. D Company, 7 Som LI's commander, Major Sydney Young, was renowned for his 'grip' of difficult situations and true to form, led a platoon forward with their hand held anti-tank weapon, the PIAT. The Battalion's historian who witnessed the action records:

'An attempt was made to deal with the enemy tank with P.I.A.Ts, but the leading troops were unable to make any headway, being pinned to the ground some seventy yards from the enemy. The leading platoon

Oosterhout

River Waal

D Coy
7 Som LI

Oosterhout Dyke road

**Attack on Oosterhout by
7 Som LI and
A Sqn 4/7 DG
22 September 1944**

JELLALABAD

129 BRIGADE

ARNHEM
NIJMEGEN

AM

A Coy
PM

B Coy
PM

Oosterhout Dyke road

C Coy

AM

D Coy

A Sqn

214 BRIGADE

RIVER WAAL

commander, Lieutenant W. Tharp, was wounded. Major Young was severely wounded while making his reconnaissance. The Commanding Officer came forward and ordered "D" Company to make use of smoke and to endeavour to withdraw the forward platoon, so that artillery fire could be brought down on the enemy.'

Private O'Connell recalls how: 'I was in the front carrier and had to pick him [Maj Young] up and drive him to the RAP where he died a few hours later. We were saddened but it was life or death and we had to move on'. The battalion history continues:

'On his return to battalion headquarters he [the CO] ordered "C" Company Group, including one troop of tanks, to move (right flanking) to an area north of the village. "C" Company moved off at 1100 hours, but by 1220 hours was held up by heavy mortar fire from an orchard.'

With C Company was a Dutch policeman, who gave them details of the German defences in the village and, as the company advanced, he 'waved happily to Dutch civilians who peered from their houses, watching the attack'.

'A number of young prisoners fell to "C" Company – so young that they must have just come from the Hitler Youth. The Dutch Policeman interrogated them, waving his revolver so violently that they were terrified, as also was Major Durie who expected to see them shot at any moment. "For four years" said the policeman "I have been ordered about by these so-and-so's. Now I am going to do the talking!"'

C Company had advanced to the north of the village but they were halted between the Oosterhout defences and enemy blocking positions along the main road. One C Company veteran recalls that,

'We were pinned down, unable to go forward or get back. Any movement we made got a burst of Spandau in reply. I remember when we eventually rejoined the battalion they were surprised to see us, as they thought we had been wiped out.'

At this point, Commander 214 Brigade, Brigadier Essame, came forward to assess the situation for himself. He decided that it was impossible to take Oosterhout without artillery support. In the following two hours, a detailed fire plan was made for the four field

7 Som LI's forming up point for the afternoon attack on Oosterhout.

Forming up point

Oosterhout Dyke Road

and one medium regiments available. Lieutenant Colonel George Taylor, waiting behind the Somersets with his battalion, 5 Duke of Cornwall's Light, Infantry, commented:

> 'One of the difficulties that had to be faced up to at this period was the limited amount of artillery ammunition available. For this reason, 7 Som LI spent a great deal of time finding out exactly where enemy strong points were located before precious ammunition could be used.'

H-Hour was set at 1430 hours but was delayed by fifty minutes while the artillery completed preparations. Therefore, at 1505 hours (H-15 minutes) the fire plan started, including infantry heavy and medium mortars. Rounds fell accurately on the carefully plotted enemy positions.

While the artillery blasted Oosterhout, A and B Companies moved south of the village under cover of the dyke. The accompanying tanks had a particularly difficult time, as they had to drive at a precarious angle along the side of the dyke, because straying too far onto the flat ground at the base was an invitation to bog down. At H-Hour (1520 hours), the companies were deployed so as to each use one of the two roads north though the village as their axis. When the artillery fire lifted onto the northern half of the village, the Somersets swept over the dyke into the orchards and houses, followed by A Squadron's Shermans. The tanks' role in this battle was to provide direct fire, when the infantry encountered resistance. A Squadron claimed three German Mark IIIs during the action and blasted entry points into defended buildings with HE shells.

Clearing a village, is normally a slow business, with sections of riflemen dealing with individual houses and buildings. However, in less than an hour, 7 Som LI had reached their limit of exploitation at the northern end of the village. The opposition had been relatively light, as the defenders were stunned by the artillery fire. Many of the Germans fled and one hundred and thirty were taken prisoner. The Somersets who had fought the SS in Normandy commented that 'some of them, uncharacteristically, were only to happy to surrender'. To the north of the village, an 88-mm gun that was causing problem for 129 Brigade, on the road to Arnhem was knocked out. By 1700 hours, Oosterhout was secure and the battle could move on. However, the Corps Artillery was down to three rounds per gun and the Division's 25-pounders were not much better off.

Writing after the event, with only the sketchiest of information, General Urquhart was dismissive of the Somersets' attempt to reach the Rhine. He complained that they had 'wasted most of a day, held up by

A Sherman belonging to 8th Armoured Brigade passes a knocked-out panzer in the Oosterhout area.

a tank and some infantry'. However, the Somersets had found out, exactly as 1 Para Brigade had, during its attempts to re-enforce the Arnhem bridge, that without artillery support, infantry could only make slow progress against enemy in prepared positions in buildings.

The Advance of 129 Brigade – 22 September

It will be remembered that as West Countrymen of 214 Brigade were attacking the enemy flank at Oosterhout:

'The Division's plan was for 129 Brigade to take over attempts to attack down the line of the Arnhem Road ... their primary purpose was to ensure the enemy's attention remained focused on the highway rather than on his flanks.'

129 Brigade, consisting of 4 Som LI and 4 and 5 Wiltshire, had been at the rear of 43rd Wessex's column, as it struggled through the traffic on Hell's Highway. The Brigade eventually arrived in Nijmegen at dawn on 22 September and waited while 214 Brigade crossed the Waal bridges. However, commanders and their 'Orders Groups', who had travelled ahead, used the time to brief their troops. Even so, it was not until 0845 hours that Lieutenant Colonel Ted Luce led 4 Wilts across the Waal, supported by tanks of B Squadron 13/18 Hussars. Major Robbins, was with the marching column:

'The bridge was being shelled, and we were to de-bus and lead over it with all speed before the mist lifted. This we did and met a company of American airborne troops [82nd] coming our way having just been relieved; it was easy to see from their red eyes and blackened, bearded

faces that they had had a hard time. However, the lively backchat, which went on between our soldiers and theirs, helped to keep our minds off the shells, which were arriving thick and fast all round the bridge and its approaches. The bridge itself, as we marched over it, envying the hurrying vehicles, seemed five miles long; it had been the scene of a sharp fight, and was strewn with Allied and German dead.'

The attack was to be along the main Arnhem road: from the point where the Irish Guards had halted the previous day. However, despite the known difficulties, the new attack was not well co-ordinated with 214 Brigade's attack on nearby Oosterhout. The effect of the pressure to reach Arnhem was evident. Again, the single road for the tanks and the close country forced 4 Wilts to attack on a single company frontage on the left, between a pylon line and the road. 4 Wilt's plan was for A Company to take the De Haar level crossing, while B Company, who were following, would expand penetration by clearing the 'Railway Triangle' and then C and D Companies would attack Elst. Once the Wiltshiremen were through the enemy positions, the other two battalions groups of 129 Brigade were to be prepared to continue the advance to Arnhem.

Lieutenant Colonel Ted Luce

At 1130 hours, after a brief bombardment, Major Parsons led A Company's advanced through the Irish Guards Group. The advance went well until they came under fire from 'enemy' seen to the left.

See map page 52

'After some delay they proved to be elements of 7 Somerset Light Infantry, who, thinking our advance to be a German counter-attack, had put down their defensive fire. These errors having been corrected, the advance proceeded, by now also under enemy mortar fire.'

The advance continued, against slight opposition, as far at the battalion's first objective: a road a thousand yards from their start line. At this point, the Germans, with interlocking arcs of fire, opened-up. 75mm HE shells burst amongst the advancing Wiltshiremen, and 20mm tracer from quads and *Spandaus* ripped through the advancing platoons, while anti-tank guns engaged the Shermans on the exposed roadway. Within minutes, the infantry were dashing for the shelter of the drainage ditches and the tanks were pulling back into cover, leaving the leading Sherman burning furiously on the road. The petrol-fuelled tanks were not referred to by the SS troops as 'Tommy cookers' without grim justification.

A Company was checked but not defeated. As Major Parsons described, his Company's two leading platoons, 7 and 8:

'... then became involved in violent close-quarter fighting in the orchards and ditches just north of this road: the enemy was in strength, well dug-in and concealed, and held his fire until point blank range. ... The action developed into desperate section battles, stalking Spandaus *up ditches, waist deep in mud and water and then trying to rush them. All such attempts failed and casualties were heavy.'*

8 Platoon failed to make much headway. Meanwhile, 7 Platoon, on the right, approached an orchard concealing well camouflaged SS infantry, via drainage ditches. Attacking from the ditch, Lieutenant Hardiman and several of his soldiers were killed while trying to break into the enemy position in the orchard 'that they only vaguely located'. The Company 2IC, Captain Bedford, came forward to find out what was going on and rallied 7 Platoon, leading the survivors forward in another attack. The Germans, however, now alert to the threat from the drainage ditches, 'hurled a barrage of grenades into it'. Captain Bedford and most of the soldiers of 7 Platoon were hit. As the history of 4 Wilts states, 'the enemy position remained intact' and 7 Platoon pulled back out of grenade throwing range. A Company's HQ and reserve, 9 Platoon, however, made progress around the left flank via a ditch and established themselves near a culvert on the road beyond the enemy held orchard. Major Parsons describes how he:

'...was convinced that 7 and 8 platoons were up level with us but to the right. I could hear a Bren gun firing so I set off, with a patrol, up a ditch to locate them. We hadn't gone far when a German tank passed by and we pressed ourselves into the side of the bank... Having nearly reached the cross-roads, I was about to climb out of the ditch to shout for 7 and 8 Platoons, when Pte Drew caught sight of four tuff looking Germans fifty yards away. Their belts could be seen stuffed with stick grenades, which was one up to them, as we had none. We both, recovering from the surprise, exchanged some pretty hurried and wild shooting. Without grenades, I decided to withdraw back to 9 Platoon. This was carried out by fire and manoeuvre in the approved manner, albeit with considerable haste. Later when the ground was in our hands, I discovered that we had penetrated a enemy company HQ location.'

Shortly afterwards, Major Parsons and 8 Platoon had an opportunity target when a German Mark IV withdrew east across their front to the Verdelust cross-roads. It was engaged and hit by a PIAT but the damaged tank limped on to the main road.

With A Company held up by the enemy, who were seemingly concentrated along the main road, Lieutenant Colonel Luce ordered B Company to reinforce A Company and fix the enemy in place, through renewed pressure. Meanwhile, C Company were committed to a left **See map page 52** flanking movement. Major Robbins led his company to the Battalion's left boundary and:

> '... apart from heavy going in the ditches, we managed to move without undue difficulty into line with A Company but found all further lines of advance heavily covered with enemy fire. When we saw two of the 13/18 Hussar's Shermans on the road to the right knocked out by tank fire from the cross-roads, we halted and dug in.'

The two Mark IVs seen earlier by Major Pasons had been re-deploying from the forward element of Knaust's *Kampfgruppe* in Oosterhout and were now dominating the main road north to Arnhem. Knaust was maintaining a coherent front between the Oosterhout and the railway line.

Major Robbins recalled that while the battalion was sheltering in the roadside ditches from the fire of two Mark IVs:

> '...a Dutch civilian on a bicycle rode cheerfully down the road from the west. Seeing us in the ditch, he waved cheerfully "Hello British Tommies!" Whatever else he had to say was lost in a heavy burst of machine gun fire from the tanks, and it was with difficulty that he too was dragged into our ditch.'

British infantrymen take cover in front of a knocked-out Mk III. Note the point of entry of the armour piercing shell just in front of the men's faces.

Despite the lack of progress by his infantry, Brigadier Mole, hearing that Oosterhout had been taken ordered 13/18 Hussars to mount a squadron attack up the road just before last light. Brigadier Mole was hoping that a bold dash forward along the road would lead to a 'sympathetic advance' for his Brigade, while the Germans were reeling from the new gap in their line. However, the enemy position had not been 'unhinged' by the fall of Oosterhout and his advance quickly came to a halt. The Squadron withdrew back to the orchards north of Lent, with four Shermans, left burning on the road, while the 'dehorsed' crews dragged their wounded back to the Wiltshire's front line. There were to be no easy solutions or lucky breaks on the main road to Arnhem.

The Dash to Driel – PM 22 September

On the left flank, following the capture of Oosterhout, events were unfolding that even General Patton would have found hard to match in terms of dash, drive and daring. Waiting all day in the area of Hof van Holland, was 5 DCLI. The CO, Lieutenant Colonel George Taylor, had established his headquarters alongside that of 7 Som LI on the dyke road near Huis Oosterhout. Here he was briefed on the desperate plight of 1st Airborne Division and had been allocated two Dukws loads of supplies, which were to be delivered across the Rhine, into the Airborne Perimeter. As the leading elements of 7 Som LI were clearing through the northern part of Oosterhout, Taylor gave:

'...the command "Advance". Prisoners many of them wounded and a pitiful sight were being brought in by the Somersets, as our 'B' Company felt its way forward through the half-shattered village. Rumours of enemy tanks [a reality not a rumour] *caused them to move off the main road and go through a tangle of gardens and orchards, which caused a slight delay and alteration in the artillery plan. Soon they were moving through the open country, clear of the village, onto their objectives – the orchards, protected by a hail of high explosives ripping up likely enemy positions. No sign of the enemy. Over the wireless I gave the order "Push on, change of plan, seize D Company's objective", thus time was to be saved.'*

At this point, Colonel Taylor had a hard decision to make. He had reliable information that two enemy tanks had been located but chose to ignore this fact, as it would probably have caused his battalion to have hesitated. There was a fleeting chance to reach the Rhine and with less than an hour of daylight, he seized the opportunity.

'My plan was reshaped and the idea of using the carriers as a piquets

[on the battalion's route] *was given up. Speed was essential or the enemy would move his reserves to close the gap; also night was fast approaching and in the dark, we would not be able to move more than a mile or so. The vital minutes were flying. I threw off my equipment and ran to the slow plodding platoon, galvanising them into action, as they came forward from the village. Soon they were all mounted on tank, carrier, or towed anti-tank gun.'*

The battle group was divided into two columns. The first consisted of A Squadron 4/7 DG and all the Battalion's armoured vehicles, with the infantry of A and D Companies hanging on where ever they could. The second column was made up of C and B Companies, squeezed into the battalion's soft skinned vehicles and the Dukws, following a couple of miles behind the armoured column.

'Off the battalion moved, tanks clanking, motors roaring – dashing headlong. Ignoring the danger of ambush and mines, they were soon in the streets of Valburg. The Dutch inhabitants, somewhat astonished at this eruption of armour and men, went wild with joy... as the column moved quickly on. The light was fading rapidly as the head of the column reached Driel, the tracks of the leading tank being blown up on a [Polish] mine at the entrance leading to the village. The journey of ten miles had been completed in under thirty minutes. We felt that even General Patton would not grumble at this!'

See map page 9 for route

However, not all was well further back down the column. Lieutenant Colonel Taylor continues:

'...very shortly afterwards a DR [motorcycle dispatch rider] came up to the Command Carrier and reported to me that enemy tanks were attacking the armoured vehicle column. He had been standing at the crossroads between Valburg and Elst to direct traffic and seeing some tanks approach he signalled them on. A few seconds later, to his horror, he saw the dark German crosses on the tanks. Fortunately, his motor cycle was just around the corner facing in the right direction and running to it, he moved to Driel with all speed to report.

'It was realised that in the darkness the troops of the column would have a good chance of holding off the tank attack. The armoured column immediately took up positions of all round defence. I then turned my attention to linking up with the airborne troops and delivering the two 'Duwk' loads of supplies.'

Signalman Stan Proctor, manning a rear radio link back to HQ 214 Brigade remembers:

Lieutenant Colonel Taylor

An infantry section mounted on the hull of a Sherman tank.

'We with 1st Worcesters, were behind 5 DCLI. As we progressed in
the dark, I heard Scotty's voice in my earphones; "I am behind a tank
which has just joined the convoy. It has a big black cross on it and I am
looking straight up the barrel of an 88mm gun".'

Meanwhile, back near the Lienden crossroads Company Sergeant
Major Philip was struggling to keep up with his company commander:

'Major Parker was leading A Company's group of vehicles in his
jeep, but he was travelling at too greater speed for my carrier and by the
time we were half way to Driel, I was 600 yards behind, and the carrier
following behind was another 200 yards away.

'In the distance, I saw Major Parker passing a tank on the fork roads between Elst and Driel, but I carried on, as I failed to realise that they were Germans. When I was within 100 yards, I saw that they were a column of tanks, and, what was more important they were all marked with black crosses. We could not stop, but charged on hoping to get through. The first two tanks pulled over to the right of the road and we skidded to a standstill with the front of the carrier touching the front of the tank. At the time, I was sitting on the top of the carrier with a light machine gun on my lap. The tank commander leaned out of the turret and removed his goggles, so I immediately gave him a burst with my LMG and he slithered down inside the turret. At the same time, the German crew opened fire with two machine guns but as one was too low

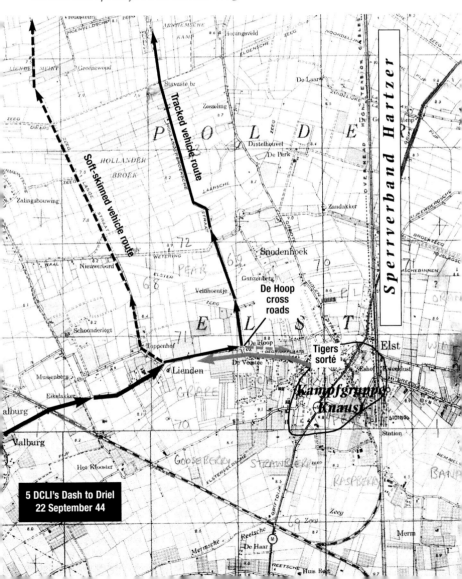

5 DCLI's Dash to Driel
22 September 44

The British infantry's answer to the mighty Tiger's 88mm gun – the PIAT.

and the other two high [the hull and turret machine guns respectively], *we did not suffer any casualties, and we all baled out to the right and left of the road. As I jumped from the carrier, I remember striking my head on the 88-millimetre gun of the tank. We were very lucky, as on each side of the road, was a ditch containing mud and reeds, which afforded excellent cover. From this ditch, I observed five Tiger Tanks on the road above us and about a dozen infantry about 100 yards away. Private Rogers and myself, using the cover afforded by the ditch and the failing light, managed to contact the remainder of the column which was in the rear, approximately one mile behind.'*

However, while passing the tanks, Major Parker had realized that they were German and, successfully evading them, caught up with the leading elements of his company. He deployed a platoons and some Battalion anti-tank guns to block the road and set about organizing a series of tank ambushes around the De Hoop crossroads with PIATs and Number 75 anti-tank mines on the enemy's likely routes back to Elst. He recounts in a letter to his CO that:

The De Hoop crossroads today. Elst has expanded since the war.

'Accordingly, we set our trap. I gave orders for complete silence and no rounds to be fired unless attacked by infantry because of the flash. PIATs were to be fired in a volley of three when given the order. No firing to take place until the leading tank had hit the mines. We now heard German Tiger tanks shooting up B Company and as this was happening a German motor [cycle] combination came up the road from Elst, presumably to contact the tanks. He literally blew up on our 75 mines. Next, we heard the tanks returning headed by a DR. He also blew up. The leading tank was firing Verey lights to light the way every 30 seconds. It was fairly obvious that they were "windy". These were the five tanks. As the first tank reached the 75 mines I gave the orders for groups Two and Three to fire. There was a tremendous explosion and six PIAT bombs hit the tank. This put him completely out of action. The next tank hit the mines and received the same treatment. The third tried to back out but hit a string of mines which had been pulled in behind it and came to a halt on the initial explosion, and every time he tried to move another mine went off. Eventually he too, was knocked out by Private Brown, who went within a few yards of the tank with his PIAT before he fired. The tank was out, but so was one of the eyes of the PIAT firer. The last words of Brown as he was put on the jeep and lost consciousness were "I don't care I knocked the bastard thing out!" It was his first action and he was proud of it. Brown was awarded the Military Medal for his gallant action.'

The other two tanks slipped into ditches, as they attempted to back out of the ambush and Sergeant Major Philip dropped grenades into the turrets to ensure that the tanks were immobilized. Thus, no less than five of the most powerful tanks of the time, out of 506 *Schwere* Panzer Battalion's fifteen Tiger I and IIs on the Island, were destroyed. This incident reveals how a few determined infantry can destroy what would be during full daylight, an overwhelmingly powerful force.

With 5 DCLI, less B Company, who had taken the soft vehicle route to avoid the Tigers, concentrated at Driel, Lieutenant Colonel Taylor reached Major General Sosabowski's 'excitable Poles'. From the start, the meeting did not go well. However, 'matters were pursued in a more traditional manner' when two officers from Headquarters 1st Airborne Division arrived at Driel. Colonel McKenzie, the divisional operations officer and Lieutenant Colonel Eddie Meyers, the Commander Royal Engineers, had been dispatched by General Urquhart across the Rhine in a two man inflatable recce boat. Their mission was to stress the desperate situation that 1st Airborne Division was in. George Taylor recalls how XXX Corps's fears were confirmed:

See map page 9

69

'They [1st Airborne] *were hemmed into a narrow perimeter just west of Oosterbeek. Their losses had been heavy, so much so that they hardly had sufficient men to man the perimeter and were in urgent need of reinforcements. They were all very short of sleep, supplies and ammunition, though in the case of the latter, it was not quite so urgent as had been reported. The enemy was in great force, and were especially strong in armour.*

'*When asked about the road-bridge at Arnhem he said the position had been in our hands, but nothing had been heard for the last 24 hours from Frost's Battalion, and it looked as if they had been overwhelmed. My first reaction was to move the Battalion and to attack the road bridge at Arnhem. This... was reluctantly abandoned, because it was felt extremely unlikely that we still held the bridge and that by now the enemy would be holding it in strength. It was necessary to try and reinforce firstly, the perimeter with men and secondly with supplies and thirdly it was also necessary to prevent the enemy getting round on the south side of the perimeter.*'

In the conference that followed, it was decided that 3 Polish Para would cross the Rhine in two man recce boats and improvised rafts provided by 1st Airborne's 4 Parachute Squadron RE. Getting the two Dukw loads of supplies across the river would have to wait, as launching two large vehicles would compromise the reinforcement. Therefore, a crossing time of 0200 hours was fixed for the Dukws. George Taylor recalled how:

'*Air photos of the river were studied with great care and the two*

A ditched Tiger photographed near the De Hoop crossroads; a victim of one of the DCLI's tank ambushes.

RASC 'Dukw' drivers, with the IO, did a recce of the obstacles and the riverbank. They were of the opinion that it was just possible, the obstacles being the narrow roads, which had ditches on both sides, the high bund and narrow dyke.'

5 DCLI marked the route and mounted patrols to protect the 'somewhat noisy' operation from enemy interference. The Assault Pioneer Platoon accompanied the Dukws, to help the large and unwieldy vehicles along the short but difficult route down to the riverbank. Despite the RASC drivers' optimism and the pioneers' efforts, the Dukws slid on the wet cobbled road of the dyke, where they stuck fast. Meanwhile, as explained by Brigadier Essame:

> *'The Polish Para's attempt to cross the river started at 2100 hours but the Sappers of 4 Para Squadron were unable to establish a pulling rope across the river. However, at 0135 hours, HQ XXX Corps received a message from 43rd Wessex Division "Contact made with 1 Airborne – Rafting supplies in progress." Sadly, the nights work was largely unsuccessful, with only fifty-five Poles reaching the Oosterbeek Perimeter before Sosabowski called the crossing off at 0300 hours. The fully alert enemy on the dominating Westerbouwing heights machine-gunned and mortared the river line. This fire would have had deadly effect in daylight, rather than being, as it was, "a mere added nuisance in the darkness".'*

Lieutenant Colonel Eddie Myers organized successive attempts to ferry the Poles across the river.

As 43rd Wessex Division gathered strength on the Rhine, the Germans reinforced the hundred-foot bluff of the Westerbouwing Heights. At one point, General Urquhart proposed to recapture Westerbouwing but for the sake of the Perimeter's defence, it was probably fortunate that he decided against the attack. Nevertheless, from XXX Corps point of view, any crossing of the river below the Westerbouwing Heights was always going to be an operation with little prospects of success.

Despite 5 DCLI's ten mile, headlong, Dash to Driel and the Poles futile efforts to battle with the river, 1st Airborne would have to wait a further twenty-four hours for renewed attempts at reinforcement and re-supply. Meanwhile, further XXX Corps artillery regiments were moving into both radio contact and firing range of Oosterbeek. From positions around Nijmegen, they continued to use scarce ammunition to blunt German attacks on the beleaguered Airborne in their defensive perimeter west of Oosterbeek.

129 Brigade on the Arnhem Road

While 5 DCLI were making their dramatic advance, 4 Wilt's attempt to reach Elst had been halted well short of the town. Consequently, 129 Brigade was ordered to expand the Waal Bridgehead on a new axis. 5 Wilts, waiting all day to drive north to Arnhem, were to dismount from their vehicles and advanced astride the Nijmegen – Arnhem railway, running parallel to the main road. Passing through the Irish Guards, 'B Company led, with platoons leapfrogging forward to the west of the high railway embankment... [until], in the darkness, came the clear sound of German voices ahead'. The battalion historian continued:

'The Company Commander decided that he had extended too far beyond the rest of the Battalion to put in an attack, and so silently the Company dug-in in the area of a signal box, having gained over a mile of valuable ground. The Germans were obviously at first unaware of their presence, for a German officer strolled down the railway line right into B Company, where he was duly captured. In the morning, it was found that the enemy were less than 50 yards away.'

Summary

On the evening of 22 September, 5 DCLI had taken one of the few opportunities presented to XXX Corps during the entire GARDEN campaign and exploited it, reaching the Rhine. Sadly, being sixty miles up a tenuously held corridor, it was an opportunity that could only ever offer limited assistance to 1st Airborne Division. Once off the main highway, away from the Arnhem Bridge, now firmly in German hands, 43rd Wessex Division had been directed into a strategic *cul de sac*, as far as continuing MARKET GARDEN was concerned. However, the Wessex Division's presence on the southern bank of the Rhine now prevented the Germans from cutting off 1st Airborne Division from the river.

This Wessex Wyvern badge was worn by Sergeant Major Burt Tremaine (5 DCLI) during the Dash to Driel.

CHAPTER FIVE

REINFORCEMENT ACROSS THE RHINE

1st Airborne Division's supply situation was poor but thanks to the bravery of the Allied aircrews of 38 and 46 Groups, some food, ammunition and medical supplies were dropped within the Perimeter. A much higher proportion fell into German hands but above all, what was needed were reinforcements. The thought of evacuation had not entered the minds of 1st Airborne, as they believed they held a viable bridgehead from which XXX Corps' could reach its MARKET GARDEN objective, the Ijsselmeer, forty miles to the north. Similarly, 43rd Wessex Division was focused on reaching the Rhine and repeating their successful assault crossing formula, used on the Seine at Vernon. Despite unaccustomed supply difficulties, British soldiers were still confident that they would succeed.

130 Brigade's Advance to the Rhine – 23 September 1944

XXX Corps's MARKET GARDEN story, is one of narrow roads and traffic jams and on 23 September, the tempo Wessex Division's operations were again reduced to 'snail's pace' by unsuitable roads. General Thomas's planed to establish a firm grip on the Rhine by

Commanding officer, Lieutenant Colonel Coad, alongside an armoured car of his tactical HQ of 5 Dorset.

sending 130 Brigade Group north, as a priority, to reinforce the Poles and 5 DCLI. Waiting to follow 130 Brigade's column, was 214 Brigade, which was to attack Elst.

At 0630 hours, in heavy autumn rain, 130 Brigade crossed onto the Island. Their route north would take them across the country between Oosterhout and Driel that was still, in effect, no man's land. 130 Brigade's move is described by Brigadier Essame, who spent most of the day at Valburg waiting for his Brigade's turn to move.

'The dawn of 23rd September came with cold and driving rain. Led by 5 Dorset, 130 Brigade was directed by the Regulating Headquarters, established by 8 Middlesex near the roundabout by the main road bridge in Nijmegen, on to the Bund and the route taken by the DCLI the previous evening. 7 Hampshire group followed 5 Dorset: then came brigade headquarters and finally 4 Dorset group. It had under its command the 13/18 Hussars and included a number of lorries carrying assault boats for the crossing of the Rhine. The brigade was mounted on Dukws. On the narrow embanked roads, these unwieldy vehicles were

Infantry and tanks advancing across the Island in the rain.

to prove a serious liability. The slightest error in driving landed them irrecoverably in the ditch. The sharp corners proved particularly difficult to negotiate as the head of the column reached the crossroads at Valburg, enemy artillery opened up. Roofs crashed down, houses were blasted and several Dukws received direct hits. Enemy tanks from the direction of Elst now opened fire and cut Lieutenant Colonel Coad's battalion, 5 Dorset, in two. He pushed on, however, with the front half and by 11.30 a.m. had reached Driel.'

XXX Corps's signal log records a message from the Wessex, at 1120 hours, that '5 DCLI report 130 Bde are arriving in their area'. The divisional historian continues his account:

'The rear of his column meanwhile proceeded to fight its way through under cover of smoke from their mortars and fire from their anti-tank guns. The infantry crawled along the ditches; the vehicles ran the gauntlet. All had joined their commanding officer in Driel by 1300 hours. A Company (Major HC Allen) was soon established on the riverbank near the broken Railway Bridge. The other two companies were disposed in an orchard with battalion headquarters about half a mile from the river... It was not until well on in the afternoon that the tail of 130 Brigade's Column bedevilled by the fire of 88s and machine guns, finally cleared Valburg crossroads. 7 Hampshire deployed on the river bank near Heteren. 4 Dorset, in reserve, took up a position at Homoet.'

No accusation of sloth can be levelled at 130 Brigade. As experienced combat troops, they pushed on to the Rhine despite the enemy's enfilading fire from the east. Even 130 Brigade's logistic echelon vehicles bravely followed on, despite the all too obvious risks.

Meanwhile, 214 Brigade was waiting to attack Elst in order to widen the route north and protect the Division's exposed eastern flank. This flank posed the most serious threat, with the Germans now able to reinforce the Island via the Arnhem Bridge. The attack on Elst by 214 Brigade will be covered Chapter 7. On the afternoon of 23 September according to plan, the Recce Regiment reinforced by 12 KRRC, deployed on to the Island and fanned out five miles to the west in a loose screen against little opposition.

The Second Polish Crossing of the Rhine – 23/24 September 1944

Following the previous night's operation, during which just fifty-five Polish paratroopers crossed the Rhine, a better-planned and resourced operation was scheduled for the evening of 23 September. The Polish Brigade (little more than battalion strength) was to be ferried across, followed by 5 Dorset and 7 Hampshire. However, only sixteen collapsible canvas and plywood assault boats were to be found in the Divisional Engineer Park. Each Mark III boat could carry sixteen assault troops. Airborne Engineer, Lieutenant Colonel Myers was now to spend a second night attempting to organize another Polish crossing. With the language difficulty and the Poles being untrained for this type of operation, Brigadier Essame records that:

> 'There were many delays in the darkness and it must be recorded that General Sosobowski's attitude was the reverse of co-operative. Enemy shelling and mortaring added to the confusion and the crossing did not start until a late hour.'

Every weapon 130 Brigade and the tanks of 13/18 Hussars could bring to bear supported the assault crossing, which was illuminated by a building set on fire by the Germans. Losses similar to those suffered by 3/504 PIR during the Waal crossing three days earlier, were suffered by the Poles. Enemy fire holed boats and a lack of watermanship skills contributed to mounting confusion. The success of Colonel Myers's second ferrying operation was limited, as he managed to ferry just 250 Poles across the river. Meanwhile, the Wessex Division's infantry spent a frustrating night, waiting their turn to cross. The operation was

Even though they were made of plywood and canvas, assault boats were remarkably heavy and difficult loads for infantry to carry.

eventually abandoned at dawn, with most of the boats left on the northern bank, where they were destroyed during the day. Unlike the daylight crossing of the Waal by 504 PIR, the crossing of the Rhine on the night of 23 September was totally lacking surprise, with German machine guns dominating the river. Again, and not for the last time, were the British and Poles to rue the loss of the vital and dominating Westerbouwing Heights.

Colonel Mackenzie was one of those who paddled across with the leading wave and made his way back to General Urquhart's headquarters in the Hartenstine Hotel, at the centre of the Oosterbeek Perimeter. As General Urquhart recorded:

> 'He was torn between telling me what Horrocks and Thomas thought was going to happen, and the contrary view he held as a result of what he had seen and heard. He was certain in his own mind now that no reinforcement of any consequence could possibly arrive in time, and he chose to gloss over this interpretation and to give me the official picture which was rosier.'

Colonel Mackenzie

The Valburg Conference – 24 September 1944

Just as the Poles' crossing was beginning at 2200 hours, a signal from General Dempsey's Second Army was received by Generals Horrocks and Browning at their co-located headquarters at Malden. The signal authorised the withdrawal of 1st British Airborne Division 'if the situation warranted it'. The events of the next few days must be measured against the background of senior officers realizing that MARKET GARDEN had failed, even if this was not yet apparent to those actually fighting the battle. With Britain's dwindling manpower resources in autumn 1944, the Principal of War of 'never reinforcing failure' was highly applicable.

On the morning of 24 September, Generals Horrocks and Thomas climbed the steps of the Driel Church tower and surprised the FOO of 220 Battery 112 Field Regiment RA. General Thomas's recollections of the discussions during their thirty minutes at the

Driel Church. The tower overlooking the Rhine, was used as an artillery OP.

top of the church tower are recorded in the divisional history:

'Lieut General Horrocks faced the facts. The position held by the Airborne Division had no military value. It was merely a nebulous area in wooded hills with very little control over the riverbank, which ran dead straight for well over half a mile. The enemy held the high ground overlooking the river and approaches to it. It would therefore be impossible to bring bridging lorries down in daylight. Even if a bridge were built it would still be under direct fire from the opposite bank above and below the bridge site. He therefore instructed 43rd Division to carry out the evacuation.'

Major General Sosabowski

A conference was called at the Wessex Division's headquarters at Valburg. Those attending, in addition to the Corps Commander and the 43rd's staff, included General Sosabowski and Lieutenant Colonel Myers. Polish Lieutenant Jerzy Dyrda, a fluent English speaker recalls:

'A runner from headquarters came up to me and said "Lieutenant you are to report immediately to the General". When I asked what was happening, the soldier replied that a British general had arrived and had an animated conversation with General Sosabowski. ...I was surprised that the General had been called to the conference at Valbourg. Horrocks, as Corps and front commander could have given Sosabowski his orders for a night crossing [at Driel]... I asked the General if the great offensive to bring relief to the A/B Div was about to begin at last. But the General just muttered something unintelligible into his moustache, so I realized that my conclusions were wrong.'

Lieutenant Gener Horrocks

General Horrocks has written about his orders given at Valburg. However, it is clear from other sources that, although he makes no mention of it, the decision to evacuate the airborne from the Oosterbeek Perimeter was already taken.

'There seemed to me to be a distinct danger that

Major General Tho

78

the airborne troops might be cut off altogether from the river. The trouble was that the Germans were holding the high ground on both sides of the airborne perimeter and could sweep the river with machine-guns firing on fixed lines, and the losses in our assault boats had been very heavy indeed. In fact, the only possibility was to cross at night under as much artillery fire as we could afford.

'I issued orders to General Thomas, commanding the 43rd Division, and to Major-General Sosabowski, commander 1st Polish Parachute Brigade:

'Firstly: In order to relieve pressure on the bridgehead, Thomas was to carry out an assault crossing that night, with at least one battalion of his own [4 Dorset], to be followed by the Poles, with as many stores as possible – particularly ammunition. This, of course, depended on how many assault-boats he could muster. I promised him the support of the Corps Artillery, though ammunition was getting dangerously short...

'Having issued these orders, I then drove back twenty-five miles towards Eindhoven to meet Dempsey at St Oedenrode. This was very necessary because I had not seen him or Monty for some days and we had reached the crisis point of the battle.'

The Valburg conference was a difficult meeting. General Sosabowski had proved to be 'far from co-operative'. This was perhaps understandable because, as far as he knew, his glider element was fighting north of the river along with around three hundred of his paratroopers who had crossed during the previous two nights. To make matters worse, Sosabowski was now being marginalized and his units were being given orders without reference to him. A very damaging personality clash was being played out during one of the worst crises of the entire Campaign. Brigadier Essame recorded a particularly bitter exchange:

'Having heard the outline of the plan, he said, "I am General Sosbowski, I command the Polish Brigade. I do as I like." Lieutenant General Horrocks and Major General Thomas exchanged glances. Then Lieutenant General Horrocks said: "You are under my command. You will do as I bloody well tell you." To this forthright statement, General Sosabowski replied: "All right. I command the Polish Para Brigade and I do as you bloody well say." The conference then continued on more formal lines.'

Lieutenant Dyrda recalls the meat of General Thomas's somewhat perfunctory orders that followed the Corps Commander's opening statement of intent:

'Thomas stated that there would be two crossings at 10 P.M. tonight.

79

A contemporary picture looking across the Rhine from the Driel Dyke Road to the German-held high ground beyond the river.

The crossing would be carried out by the 4th Dorsetshire Battalion at the Driel / Heveadorp ferry crossing. The Dorsets would take supplies, ammunition and food for the 1st Airborne Division on the other side of the river. At the same time, 10 P.M., the remaining units of the 1st Polish Parachute Brigade were to cross using the crossing point used on

Polish officers discuss details with officers of 4 Dorset following the Valbourg Conference.

the previous nights. The overall commander for both crossings was to be Brigadier Walton, commanding officer of 130 Brigade.

'When General Thomas had finished, I was staggered by his short perfunctory speech. He had not given any information needed for organizing the crossings. There was no explanation; how many boats; of what type and when they would arrive and who would row them, Engineers or the Parachutists themselves? What about the artillery support direct or indirect, or would the British tanks cover the crossings? And many other questions. In particular, what was to happen next? When would the great offensive take place? And the worst thing of all was that no British officer asked questions. Everything was clear and obvious to them.'

With part of his Brigade already committed in the Oosterbeek Perimeter, General Sosabowski was still not prepared to accept a low-level reinforcement operation as a prelude to an evacuation. He believed that a divisional scale operation was required to reinforce 1st Airborne Division and that this might change the fortunes of Operation MARKET GARDEN. He was not to know that there was no possibility of sufficient engineer equipment or ammunition being assembled in sufficient time to mount such an operation. There is an abiding suspicion that the Valburg conference was not so much designed by Generals Horrocks, Browning and Thomas to impart information to subordinate commanders, as to deal with Sosabowski's insistence that XXX Corps cross the Rhine in force.

4 Dorset's Crossing of the Rhine – Night 24/25 September 1944

Operational security meant that the commander's intent to evacuate 1st Airborne the following night could not be passed down the ranks of 4 Dorsets. Consequently, to this day, veterans of 4 Dorset are divided as to the actual aim of their crossing. However, on 24 September, most all

The view across the Rhine to Westerbouwing showing how far the majority of 4 Dorset was set down stream.

of them believed that they were to reinforce the 1st Airborne Division, thus continuing MARKET GARDEN. This minor deception was necessary to preserve security should a Dorset be taken prisoner. However, the company commanders, in a battalion that had been virtually destroyed in its first battle on Hill 112 in Normandy, understood that 4 Dorset was to be committed as a 'forlorn hope'. Major Phillip Roper of C Company recalled the Orders Group in the Driel church tower:

'We could see everything up to the trees which came down to the edge of the river on the north bank, but nothing in the trees on the ground which sloped steeply upwards from the river. Colonel Tilly said, "Gentlemen, we've bought it this time." I think he realized it was a pretty hairy operation. As for myself, I thought it unlikely we would get back. When I had my company O-Group I tried to water it down as much as possible and told them we were going to do an important job to help the airborne people.'

Proceeded by a twenty minute bombardment by the divisional artillery, 8 Middlesex's MMGs and heavy mortars, and the 13/18 Hussars, the Dorsets crossing was to be launched at the site of the scuttled ferry. At the same time, the Poles were to cross into the Perimeter, using their previous crossing site. 4 Dorset's objective was to secure the area surrounding a large factory some six hundred metres north of the riverbank. H-Hour was to be 2200 hours, as rainfall upstream would significantly increase the current after midnight, which would set the assault boats downstream, dispersing them over a long stretch of the

82

Westerbouwing Ferry

Oosterbeek Perimeter

Intended Polish crossing site →

northern bank. Despite the conviction amongst the senior element of the battalion that they were reinforcing a failure, the plan and fire support sounded impressive to the ordinary soldier. Private Pollitt said, 'When they talked about corps and divisional artillery, we expected the usual deafening row. In the event, the fire was deafening but later it seemed to me that at least 50% of it was German coming in our direction!'

The one vital piece of equipment, the assault boats, did not arrive on time. The usual battalion's worth of thirty boats and some Class 40 Ferries had been dispatched up Hell's Highway from the engineer field parks with an 'absolute priority' and a military police escort. However, once on the still tenuously held Island, two of the five truck loads of boats and the ferries missed a tac-sign and drove into enemy held Elst. A further two trucks slid off the dyke road into drainage ditches and stuck fast. Eventually, a mere five boats arrived with the Poles at Driel, which Brigadier Walton commandeered for 4 Dorset, when he observed a repetition of the previous night's confusion. Meanwhile, more of the unwieldy Dukws, carrying combat supplies for 1st Airborne, came to grief on the Island roads and were lost in ditches and to enemy fire. Lieutenant Colonel Henniker, the Commander Royal Engineers, recently posted from 1st Airborne Division, wrote to CO 4 Dorset after the battle:

'We only met for a few moments in the dark in that orchard where your start line was, for crossing the middle Rhine. I joined the Division the day before. After that frantic box-up, in every possible way, your last

83

words to me were "Tell the Brigadier that everything is OK. Thank him for his arrangements." Everything went wrong. You paid the price. You need have no qualms about emphasising the Sappers' failure.'

Lieutenant Colonel Tilley did not blame Lieutenant Colonel Henniker or the Sappers. He and the rest of the Division knew that his battalion had been asked to achieve the impossible, against an enemy who were ready and awaiting another crossing. The Germans had reinforced Westerbouwing with additional machine guns and fire trenches were dug along the bluff to cover the river and its banks. In the pouring rain and confusion of battle, Colonel Henniker was seen on the fire swept riverbank as dawn rose. Captain Hall of 4 Dorset recalls:

'I saw the CRA and CRE in their white macs, soft hats and swagger canes walking up and down discussing what they could do to help. A wonderful [and brave] *British sight!'*

Of the twenty assault boats that eventually arrived with the Dorsets, eight were allocated to each of the leading companies, with four boats going to Battalion Headquarters and supporting elements. The assault boats were crewed by three Sappers from 204 and 553 Field Companies, who, in theory, could each take ten infantrymen. With a company's allocation of boats, able to carry only a hundred or so troops in the each crossing, two flights would be required to get A and B Company groups across the river. With the Rhine's current increasing rapidly, it was clear, in hindsight, that the companies would be extremely unlikely to be able to concentrate for a concerted advance. If the initial attack went well, C and D Companies would follow, with S (fire support) Company Headquarters organizing the ferrying of supplies into Perimeter.

The crossing did not begin until 0100 hours, when the current was at its fastest. However, with time and the cover of darkness passing quickly, the Dorsets had no option but to mount the assault. Major Mike Whittle commanding B Company explained:

'After a long cold wait in the pouring rain, we moved forward with the boats. The whole foul night was illuminated by the light of a blazing factory, set alight by the Germans, 400 yards down stream. Once we were in the water, we were nicely silhouetted for the Germans on the bank above us. There weren't enough paddles and the first two boats were swept downstream. The remainder of my boats, about, six, had to use spades as well in order to maintain direction. Even so, we were swept downstream and landed about one hundred yards above the burning factory with two other boats. We appeared to have landed beyond the main German positions, as there was little opposition to

Soldiers of 4th Battalion the Devonshire and Dorset re-enact the crossing carried out by their forebears during the Fiftieth Anniversary Commemorations.

start with. I understand that three boats following were badly holed before they reached the water, one boat eventually landed well below the burning factory and two sunk during the crossing. The men were heavily laden, with no life jackets and most of my losses [missing in action] *came from the platoons that manned these boats.*

'With less than a quarter of my Company [two officers and about thirty-five men] *I moved across a flat piece of land to some trees about fifty yards away at the foot of a steep hundred foot escarpment. We attacked up the bank and immediately met heavy enemy resistance. Grenades came rolling down the hillside and caused us many casualties. I eventually reached the top of the bank to see the Germans withdrawing. We briefly occupied their slit trenches and, having lost fifty percent of our small force, we did not pursue them. Instead, I followed the top of the bank to the east in an attempt to get in touch with A Company.*

'The CO came up behind us with a boatload of C Company under Major Roper. Together they set of inland towards the Battalion's objective. They advanced with the CO leading. They were soon surrounded and the CO shouted "There they are boys: get at them with the bayonet." An hour and a half after that, just before first light, they were forced to surrender. We soon ran into more trenches and were unable to reach Major Grafton and A Company.'

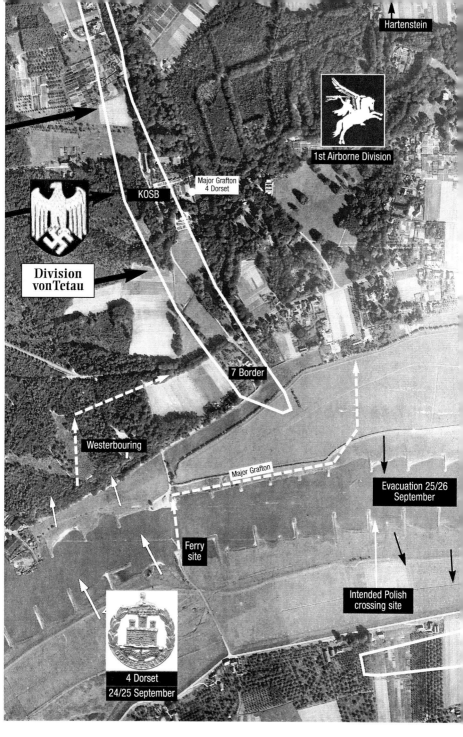

Hartenstein

1st Airborne Division

Major Grafton
4 Dorset

KOSB

Division
vonTetau

7 Border

Westerbouring

Major Grafton

Evacuation 25/26
September

Ferry
site

Intended Polish
crossing site

4 Dorset
24/25 September

9th SS Hohenstaufen Panzer Division

Lonsdale Force

Oosterbeek Church (Captain Rose RA)

R H I N E

Railway Bridge (blown)

5 Dorset 23 Sept/4 Oct

Pte Mathews, a C Company signaller, described his nightmare crossing and his subsequent capture:

'We started to cross the river but a mortar shell hit the first boat, two comrades were wounded and had to be evacuated. We tried again later in a second boat, halfway over the officer i/c shouted "Turn back". He was wounded and the boat riddled with shrapnel and bullet holes. We then transferred to another boat for the third time. The major was wounded but refused to be left behind. After many minutes of horror, toil and sweat, reached the opposite side. "Duce", the company runner and I started to make our way to the RV through dense woods in absolute darkness. We suddenly stopped, looking down the barrels of German rifles. I quickly turned the tuning dials off frequency on the radio set. We were blindfolded and marched away to a house. I was terrified. After being interrogated and asked many questions, all our personal belongings were taken away. We were thrown into a cellar and left for several hours frozen stiff. The Jerries gave us some water and tiny pieces of bully beef.'

Private Aubrey Steirn, also of C Company fared little better:

'At first light, we decided to move further into the woods in an attempt to gain contact with other members of the battalion. I was in the lead when a machine gun opened up on me from a very short distance. I was knocked over and remember, in what must have been seconds of unconsciousness, my past floating by and thinking I was too young to die. Obviously I was, because I came to in one piece, apart from a facial wound and a badly bruised shoulder where a burst of fire had "clipped" me and left metal fragments in my uniform. In the meantime, the Germans had been dealt with, and we then moved on and encountered more fragments of the unit, including the CO. We occupied German trenches in the area and continued to operate until completely surrounded.'

Many Dorsets, spread out along hundreds of yards of river bank, suffered a similar fate; being overwhelmed during the course of the day, as they fought their way inland to their objectives in small groups. About three hundred Dorsets and supporting arms crossed the Rhine, with the operation being called off only when there were no boats left intact.

A Company had fared worse than any other company. Major Grafton's boats crossed directly under the strongest portion of the enemy defences. His first boat was set on fire by tracer, while it was being man handled down to the river and he had to find a place for himself and his three man tactical HQ in another boat. During post-

Present-day Devon and Dorset recruits following in the steps of the 4 Dorset find it hard going up the bluff from the Rhine to Westerbouwing (and they weren't under fire and in darkness).

operational debriefing Major Grafton said 'I looked up and around when we were about half way across the river. We were alone. The rest of my company had seemingly disappeared.'

Major Grafton reached the jetty on the northern bank exactly where planned and 'came under fire from machine guns to our immediate front and left flank'. Realizing that his single boatload of Dorsets, numbering no more than twenty men, could not reach the objective on its own, they remained in the area waiting for others until 0345 hours. The accompanying forward observation officer from 112 Field Regiment RA, Captain Zeke Rose, called down artillery fire on German positions on the bluff. When it was clear that they were separated from the remainder of the battalion, Major Grafton led his party to the Perimeter. Accompanying him was Lieutenant Eccles, who was carrying a second copy of General Browning withdrawal orders. By following the riverbank to the east, they avoided an enemy position and reached 1st Airborne. Lieutenant Eccles went on to Divisional Headquarters and having handed over the orders for Operation BERLIN, he made his way back to join Major Grafton. Altogether, some eighty Dorsets and one of the two FOO parties joined the Airborne Division fighting in the Perimeter.

See air photo p86-87

Back on the river bank Major Whittle could not locate anyone from A Company.

'It was now almost light, so we returned to the landing point where

I found about twenty others. I called in the remainder of B Company, we searched for others in the nearby trees and I gave the order to dig in behind a bank half way between the river and the trees. On checking up, I discovered my strength to be about thirty, comprising a few men of B, C and D Companies, about ten of S Company and an MO and quartermaster belonging to the Airborne Forces.

'We remained in this position throughout the day. Our trenches were continually being fired on by snipers on the top of the bank among the trees and a German patrol made an attempt to attack us. The Germans were lobbing grenades from their positions thirty yards away in the edge of the wood. They were shouting out "Hey you Tommy – why don't you surrender? Hands up. Hands up!" One stalwart replied by sending shots into the wood and shouting to them in the loudest voice he could "get packing!" There were several casualties from snipers and MG fire, and also from a well-meaning couple of Spitfires which "Strafed" us. A German speaking reasonably good English did his best to make us surrender.*

'After dark that night* [25/26 September] *German patrol activity*

A heavy mortar section (4.2-inch) belonging to 8 Middlesex ready to provide fire support.

became very active, and one group was located infiltrating along the riverbank behind us. I therefore gave the order to withdraw to the riverbank. One man, a strong swimmer, volunteered to try and get back to Brigade Headquarters for further orders. We waited another hour and a half during which time, we had several skirmishes with enemy patrols, and about 2300 hours I decided to withdraw across the river. We had found one sound boat and the wounded and non-swimmers were pushed off in this; the rest of us swam back. I arrived back at Brigade Headquarters in Driel with fifteen men at 2330 hours.'

Of 4 Dorset's two hundred and thirteen losses attributable to the operations on 24 to 26 September 1944, many were PWs but a high proportion were lost in the Rhine. There are only fifteen known 4 Dorset graves on the northern riverbank. This attempt to reinforce or relieve 1st Airborne Division contributed to 4 Dorset's unenviable record of being the battalion with the highest number of soldiers listed as 'Missing in Action' in the entire North West European Campaign.

XXX Corps's Fire Support – 25 September 1944

The presence of 4 Dorset on the riverbank distracted German attention from the weakly defended western flank of the Airborne Perimeter. However, Captain Rose and his FOO party, having reached the Perimeter, played an importance and largely unrecognized part in ensuring the Perimeter's survival. Also available was Major Grafton's A Company Tactical Headquarters, with its vital radios and the even more important signal instructions. Armed with this document, he was able to speak directly to Battalion Headquarters and other divisional fire support units. Captain Zeke Rose of 477 Battery was sent from the Hartenstein to join 1st Airborne Light Regiment RA, at the Oosterbeek Church. Here artillery fire was being co-ordinating against 9th SS Panzer Division, which was increasing pressure on the Perimeter's eastern flank. Captain Rose was able to help by calling for the divisional artillery's full weight of fire. For example, his direct communication with his CRA speeded up the passage of fire orders and consequently multiplied the fire effect, by more than doubling the number of fire missions possible in a given period. Major Phillip Tower, an officer on 1st Airborne Division's artillery staff, praised Captain Rose for his invaluable support, 'culminating in a Mike target [Regimental shoot] on the Light Regiments HQ, at the time surrounded by German infantry and three Tiger tanks'. Captain Rose was killed later that day. Airborne Gunner, Lieutenant Frank Moore, who commanded the airborne 75mm guns dug in nearby recalls that they were at his CP in the Church porch and:

> *'Zeke was standing next to me, while I pointed out enemy mortar and machine gun positions. He was hit by a burst of MG fire but I was not. He was put in the church where he said he was not in pain. I am not sure if he died there or later in hospital.'*

Captain Rose's Bombardier assistant continued to call down 43rd Division's fire throughout the night. Many Arnhem veterans bitterly resent the delayed arrival of XXX Corps. However, few have anything but praise for the artillery that supported them in the Perimeter.

Major Grafton and the mixed bag of eighty Dorsets were sent to reinforce the thinly spread 7 KOSB, who were holding the western flank against the growing strength of Division von Tetau. At this stage of the battle, eighty infantrymen represented a significant reinforcement to the hard-pressed Scotsmen. Rather than adjusting positions in daylight to give the Dorsets their own sector to hold, they were sent to the 'companies' in groups of ten. In addition, Major Grafton called down mortar fire and, through 130 Brigade, called for artillery fire. Lieutenant Douglas Goddard, Gun Position Officer of 220 Battery recalls that:

> *'Major Grafton, 4 Dorset, who was with the A/B pocket called over the radio for an arty concentration to be laid on the spot he was occupying to disperse tanks which had penetrated between two groups of Paras [KOSB]. The fire was effective, as were other concentrations he called down before German pressure forced them to destroy the radio and withdraw.'*

Small though the Dorset's infantry reinforcement was, two channels of direct radio communication to their Wessex Division's fire support units, was a contribution that helped the Paratroopers hold on until the evacuation that evening.

The porch of Oosterbeek Church where Captain Zeke Rose was killed on 25 September 1944.

CHAPTER SIX

THE EVACUATION OF 1st AIRBORNE DIVISION – OPERATION BERLIN

Planning and Preparation – 25 September 1944

Despite Lieutenant General Horrocks's description of his intentions to reinforce the Oosterbeek Perimeter, a decision had been taken before the Valburg Conference on 24 September, in principal, to evacuate 1st Airborne in Operation BERLIN. This information was confined to a few senior British officers but Horrocks had to travel back down Hell's Highway to confer with General Dempsey, before finally authorising the evacuation. 4 Dorset's Rhine crossing had been designed to secure a firmer grip on the river bank in order to facilitate the evacuation, not to reinforce the Perimeter. The cut of Hell's Highway at Kovering, in 101st Airborne Division's area, brushed aside lingering doubts over the viability of Montgomery's plan.

Amongst those summoned forward were Storm Boats and Canadian crews from the Army Group Royal Engineers, who were to

General Horrocks (with map) travelled south down Hell's Highway to St Oendenrode to confer with General Dempsey.

supplement 43rd Wessex Division's RE Field Companies. However, as the following entries, dated 25 September, in XXX Corps log indicate, not all the trucks were able to get through

'1320 hrs. Assault boats are at the head of the column behind the block. [on Hell's Highway at Koevering].

'1430 hrs. The road is now almost clear and things are going well. 7 Armd Div are clearing from SOUTH under Comd 50 Div and hope to clear it soon.

'1705 hrs. 50 Div report unlikely road situation will clear up before 0900 tomorrow [26 September].'

Without a full compliment of boats, Operation BERLIN was going to be difficult and more protracted affair than was originally planned.

The closure of Hell's Highway also had implications for the artillery. Without a regular supply of ammunition from the rear, fire missions in support of 1st Airborne and the barrage to cover the evacuation, would again reduce ammunition stocks dangerously low levels. This was a risk that had to be taken.

Most of the fire planning was conducted by 1st Airborne north of the Rhine. Located in exposed gun positions on the Island, 112 Field Regiment's historian wrote:

'A massive Fire Plan Task Table was prepared by the A/B Div Arty staff officers, Major Phillip Tower and Lt Paddy de Burgh, to cover the evacuation. It was passed partly by Slidex [a fiddely battlefield radio code] *over the Gunner* [radio] *net to the CCRA, 30 Corps, and partly via the 1 A/B Div Arty FOU, Major Reggie Wight-Boycott, who swam back across the river.'*

General Urquhart said 'that we expect much from the gunners shooting from the Island'. His Commander Royal Artillery, replied 'I'm sure we'll get all we want'. Despite the looming shortage of ammunition, the Gunners planed to put down heavy barrages to prevent the Germans discovering that the paratroopers were withdrawing by covering noise and movement. This worked admirably and was supplemented by pouring rain and a very dark night.

Much of the evacuation's planning fell to Lieutenant Colonel Myers to whom, according to General Urquhart:

'... fell the dual responsibility of selecting the routes and fixing the ferry service. He had hardly recovered from his ordeal of crossing the river in

Major General Urquhart

both directions only a little time before. Yet he managed to look extremely alert and he was, as usual, full of ideas. There was no need to underline just how vital were his technical experience and his qualities of character to the Division's survival.'

Two mine-taped routes were marked down to the river with glider pilots as guides at important junctions.

On the southern bank of the Rhine, 43rd Wessex Division was preparing crossing sites and points for the reception of the evacuees. 130 Brigade would command the evacuation, with the CRE, Lieutenant Colonel Henniker, co-ordinating ferrying operations, with his opposite number Lieutenant Colonel Myers controlling the northern bank. Divisional troops would take responsibility for the evacuees once they reached Driel. Meanwhile, 129 Brigade would mount a deception operation, near Heteren, several miles to the west. The 43rd's divisional historian recorded that:

'This consisted of a motley column of mortar and carrier platoons, a machine gun platoon, a number of empty Dukws, pontoon and bridge lorries under control of 5 Wilts. As dusk approached, it moved ostentatiously to the village of Heteren on the banks of the river and opened up for one hour with Bren guns, machine guns and mortars on the far bank. This deception undoubtedly ... contributed to the success of the withdrawal.'

Four Royal Engineer field companies were to carryout the ferrying. At the eastern crossing site, opposite the centre of the Perimeter, were the Wessex Division's 206 Field Company, with sixteen collapsible canvas assault boats, and 23 Canadian Field Company. The Canadians were equipped with the much more robust wooden Storm Boats, fitted with outboard engines. Major Tucker of 23 Company recalled the difficulty of getting his fourteen boats to the river.

See aerial photo on page 86

'Two floodwalls blocked the path from the off loading area to the launching sites. The first of these was about 20 feet high with banks sloping to about 45 degrees, the second was about half the height and the slope much less severe. These obstacles became most difficult to negotiate. The heavy rain softened the ground and the churning of men's feet, as they struggled over with the storm boats, soon created a slippery mess, which lent no footing whatsoever. Hand ropes were fixed, but even with these the going was extremely difficult.'

About a half a mile downstream to the west 533 Field Company and 20 Canadian Field Company, mounted a similar operation at the Driel-Hevadorp Ferry site. It had been assumed that 4 Dorset's operation had been a success and that the base of the Perimeter had been widened.

Operation BERLIN – Night 25/26 September 1944

Brigadier Essame described the actual operation:

'A reconnaissance party under Lieutenant Bevan went forward from the assembly area over a high bank and two or three ditches and taped the way to the embarkation point. On the far bank, the burning factory cast a light over the dark swirling waters of the river. Sustained and accurate machine gun fire from the direction of the Railway Bridge up river, clipped the near bank

'At nine o'clock, the whole divisional artillery opened up with overwhelming effect, tracer from the LAA Regiment marking the flanks of the crossings. A and C Companies of 8 Middlesex thickened up the fire [with heavy mortars and MMGs]. The noise was deafening and awesome as the first parties of Sappers carried the assault boats over the dyke walls and down to the water's edge. The crews dipped their oars and disappeared into the darkness. More boats followed. Punctually at 9.40 p.m. the first reached the far side and waited for the Airborne troops who were due at ten. ... Soon the first flotilla had brought across about a hundred men and some wounded, and returned to the north bank.'

SS-*Hauptsturmführer* Müller was on the receiving end of the barrage:

'... the artillery bombardment intensified; explosions followed almost without let up. The earth was trembling and a curtain of fire and dirt of hitherto unknown dimensions rose over and between our positions. We ducked down and sought shelter but we still remained exposed to the

A flash from a 5.5 inch medium gun lights up the night sky.

blind raging of the shells. Houses burned brightly and collapsed; tree tops splintered; and the new impacts dealt death and destruction.'

Sergeant Fred Petrie was with 533 Field Company, strengthening a bridge across a canal, when the call came to move north to the river. He recalled that:

'My platoon was given the task of taking the first boat across. Normally a crew of two would have been enough but I took three men with me because of the strong winds and the expectation of a swift current. Initially two assault boats were to be put in the water on the Company's front, the first boat at 21.30 hours, was timed to arrive on the far bank ten minutes later. The boats were to ply back and forth until forty minutes after midnight.

'The night was pitch black and there was a strong gusting wind with occasional heavy showers of rain. A dozen or so Sappers heaved the boat on to their shoulders and carried it through an orchard to the top of the river bank, the way being marked by white tapes. We were heartened by the gunfire of the divisional artillery firing over our heads intermixed with the business-like sound of the Vickers machine guns of the Middlesex Regiment. On reaching the river's flood bank we became aware of the return fire from the enemy side of the river, including tracer bullets. We slithered and stumbled our way from the high bank down to the water's edge, where we seemed to be below the line of fire, although an occasional mortar bomb dropped in the river behind us. Inky blackness prevailed in all directions except for the artillery flashes and the glow of a fire downstream.

'My boat having been made ready, we quickly pushed off, the crew paddling side by side in a kneeling position, with me in the bow. The current immediately took control and within seconds, we were swept downstream. The limits of the ferrying sites were marked by Bofors anti-aircraft guns firing tracer shells on a low trajectory. I was not aware of this fact at the time of the first of my crossings, otherwise I would not have been alarmed at our position directly under the line of these shells, the current having swept us to the extreme edge of the ferrying site. Only by strenuous efforts were we able to set the craft back on line for the far bank.

'Several times we were hailed by men floating or swimming past, some shouting "Tommy". At first, I wondered what were Germans doing in the water, then I realized that some of the men must have been from the Polish Parachute Brigade.

Artist's impression of the evacuation of 1st Airborne Division.

Any thoughts of attempting to pick them out of the water were quickly stifled by the fear of capsizing the boat, and, moreover, my orders were to reach the other side of the river, so we paddled on.

'A large burning building to our left cast sufficient reflected light on the water to show the nearness of the enemy bank and we also then saw flashes and came under automatic fire from straight above and ahead. As soon as the boat grounded, we jumped into the water and took cover behind a groyne until the firing stopped. ... Anxious calling brought no response ... Being concerned by the fact that our craft had been carried downstream we waded back into the river and with some difficulty pushed the boat against the current ... until we came across a Dukw stranded half on the bank. A quick investigation revealed two soldiers

hiding in side. ... they knew nothing of any other men ... it was time for us to return ... the paddles of the crew being supplemented by passengers using spades or trenching shovels.'

Subsequent trips were more successful as the boat crews learnt to 'aim off' for the current. Sergeant Fred Petrie received the Military Medal for his work in directing boats and leading by example during the evacuation.

Lieutenant Colonel Henniker was waiting on the bank:

'For a long time nothing happened. I paced the shore like a cat on hot bricks, oppressed by most gloomy forebodings. Had they upset the boats and all gone silently to the bottom, weighed down by steel helmets and rifles? Had they rowed straight into the waiting Hun on the far bank?

*Or had they merely been washed downstream to God knows where? ...
Across the dark waters came the sound of dipping oars. Then I saw a
boat. It held about a dozen men and I could see airborne pattern helmets.
Never before was there a more welcome sight. First, one boat, then
another, then another. About a hundred men came silently ashore with
a few wounded. The boats stole back into the night. ... More and more
boats were launched and then I heard the motors of the Canadian storm
boats start. No music could have seemed more sweet. Soon there was a
steady stream of men filing back along the tapes.'*

With their outboard motors, the Canadians in their Storm Boats were
able to make frequent trips directly across the river and, consequently,
evacuated the majority of those who escaped from the Perimeter.

Watching the river from the area of the Westerbouwing Heights was
a *Kriegsmarine* unit, *Sciffsturmbateilung* 10. They mistook the British
intentions and reported renewed attempts at reinforcement. Von
Tetau's diary recorded:

*'In the sector of Kampfgruppe Knoche on the lower Rhine front the
enemy made renewed crossing attempts from opposite the 10 SS, which
were mostly repelled by concentrated fire. Only individual boats
managed to cross and infiltrate. The crews were eliminated or captured
during the course of the morning.'*

The boats that the *Kriegsmarine* saw, were those that had been set
downstream by the swiftly flowing current. It is clear from SS
Obersturmbannführer Harzer's report in 9th SS *Kampfgruppe's* war diary
that even well after midnight, the Germans were unsure of what was
really happening.

As already observed by Sergeant Petrie, some paratroopers made

**Watermanship training under perfect conditions. The reality on
the Rhine was very different.**

their way to safety by swimming the fast flowing Rhine. Glider pilot Louis Hagen, was one of them. He describes the wait for the assault boats.

'We reached the banks of the Rhine and joined a long queue of men waiting to be ferried across. .... There were at least one hundred men in front of us and no sign of a boat. ... The splash of oars could be heard now and then, I suppose this was how they felt at Dunkirk. A small rowing boat was approaching at last. It took ten men across. Then we realized our desperate position. There was no cover at all and we crouched in the deep squelchy mud; we were frozen with cold and soaked from the rain.

'I began surveying our position. ... those who ordered us to wait in line for those ridiculous little boats didn't know what they were doing. The Rhine was only a hundred yards wide. Why was the order not given for those who could swim to dump their arms and make for the other side? ... But instead we were being heroic, playing at Dunkirk...

'I had to get out of this. I told Captain Z that I couldn't stand this any longer and that I was going to try and swim for it ... He agreed with me and shouted to the rest of our glider pilot section. A large crowd followed ... after us as at least we seemed to have a plan... We proceeded to take our boots off and hung them round my necks ... and in I went. The water was pleasantly warm; the air filling my battle smock kept me easily afloat. Captain Z was ... drifting fast downstream. The current was very strong, and I tried hard to reach the bank opposite. ... As my battle smock gradually deflated swimming became harder and harder. Then, I wasn't doing proper strokes any more, and I began to panic. ... I turned over on my back to rest and pull myself together. ... I had to get rid of my Sten gun. I let myself sink vertically .... Next, I methodically rid myself the impedimenta that my battle smock contained. The difference was marvellous. I swam on alone ... and the mortaring was still going on.

'I was about twenty yards from land when I saw two figures gesticulating wildly and heard shouting: "Hold on, mate, hold on, we'll be there in a moment. Don't panic, its OK, you're safe now." ... I shouted to them not to bother and that I was perfectly all right.'

Canadian Major Tucker supervising 23 Squadron's operations recalled:

'I found it impossible to keep records of the crossings made and passengers carried. Paper turned to pulp in the driving rain. It was impossible to regulate the number of passengers. Men panicked and *stormed the boats ... The maximum lift was thirty-six.'*

Major General Urquhart's crossing at the easterly site, just after midnight, in a Canadian storm boat was not without drama, thanks to a temperamental outboard motor:

'We were about halfway over when the engine gave out. There was an urgent exchange between the ferryman and one of our party and there were confused efforts to restart the engine. The boat drifted in the strong current. It was only for a few minutes, but it seemed an absolute age before we were on our way again. From the din and the great flashes of light it was obvious that the XXX Corps gunners were doing a powerful job and that they were probably making all the difference between a catastrophic evacuation and a successful one. High up on Westerbouwing there were flashes from where the Germans were firing indiscriminately on the expanse of water below.

'Suddenly the boat bumped alongside a groyne, veered round and a voice croaked, "All right. Lets be havin' you." We climbed out, sinking in the ooze.'

Fourteen stone General Urquhart had another indignity to suffer, when his braces snapped, as he scrambled up the slippery bank from the mud and met Colonel Henniker, who with 'his steel helmet and cape gleaming with rain, welcomed him'. General Urquhart's ADC recalled that his commander accepted this welcome 'holding up his trousers with irritated dignity'.

Major Geffory Powell of 156 PARA, was one of those who crossed to safety in a slower but arguably more reliable assault boat.

'When one of the boats reached the far bank, its passengers heaved themselves out of it into the water, and then pushed it back into the stream to start yet another journey. It was no place to linger, but often the men paused to shout a word of thanks to the crew before making for the high dyke they could see ahead of them.... Scrambling up its steep face, they tumbled down to the comparative safety of the far side. It was as though a curtain had dropped behind them. They were alive.'

Lieutenant Colonel Payton-Reid, Commanding Officer of 7 KOSB recalled:

'Wonder of wonders, we were on the south bank-safe and sound. Once there, it seemed as though a haven had been reached and despite mud and fatigue, all trudged four miles to Driel [it was in fact less than a mile] *with a light heart ... Until now, I had always thought exaggerated these scenes on the cinema screen, depicting the staggering and stumbling of worn-out men, but now I found myself behaving in exactly that manner ...'*

Private Gould of 1 Worcester, was helping at Driel and the state of many of the airborne made an unforgettable impression on him:

'As they passed through our ranks at Driel they looked like stunned zombies and one wondered if such devastated men would ever recover their sanity and respect. For them at least a respite, but for us the battle would go on. They had been in a very severe battle but it had lasted a mere nine days. Whereas those of us who fought on – some of us at any rate – had already endured three months of continual action and were to endure another six months before there was any respite.'

Not all were 'devastated' or lacking 'sanity and respect'. Geoffrey

Blown Rail Bridge

Rail Bridge

Royal Engineers' Memorial

The Dyke Road near the easterly evacuation point then and now.

The house was used by the Poles and the Wessex.

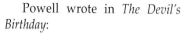

Powell wrote in *The Devil's Birthday*:

'Short though the distance was [to Driel], it was hard to summon up the strength and willpower for this final challenge. Some men shambled off down the path in twos and threes. Others collapsed after a mile or so by the side of the track. But most, clinging to the lifeline of their discipline, kept together in their groups, some even marching in step. One fifteen-man remnant of a parachute battalion arrived at Driel marching to attention in threes, with their rifles at the slope, just as if they were returning to their barracks in England: it was disciplined pride of this calibre that had kept them together through the eight-day battle.'

In his forward to the same book, Brigadier John Hackett added, 'What the author does not tell you is that this 'company' was his own. It was Geoffrey Powell who brought it out like that'.

At 0250 hours, XXX Corps received a message that 'General Urquhart has just come through. Everything seems to be going well. No news from 4 Dorset' and at '0500. OC Collecting Point reports, 1,700 men now withdrawn SOUTH of river.'

Reception at Driel

D Company 5 Dorsets were controlling the reception at the easterly crossing point. Major Hartwell recalls:

'The tremendous difficulties of the evacuation of the Airborne can hardly be imagined. No lights could be used and the night was so dark that men had to walk in front of the vehicles and they could scarcely be seen by the drivers. Many vehicles slipped off the narrow roads into the ditch and had to be overturned in order to keep the way clear. Torrential rain was falling all the time and the enemy continued to harass the area with shell and mortar fire. ... D Company was kept very busy regulating the flow of traffic. At one time 150 exhausted casualties were laying in the Company area and my men did an admirable work in comforting and evacuating them.'

The evacuees, as described by the Wessex's historian:

'... were quickly and effectively passed back to a large barn at Driel lit by the headlights of a jeep, where blankets and rum, tea and hot stew awaited them. Outside in an orchard, Lieutenant Colonel McCance, the AQMG, had ready forty jeeps equipped with stretchers, for only jeeps could master the narrow, slippery roads back from Driel. The barn and its cellars were soon full of wounded. Many of whom had discarded their

One of the barns at Driel used to receive the evacuees.

clothes to swim the river, and the houses had to be ransacked to provide covering for them.'

Major Geffory Powell recalls the scene at one of the reception centres:

'In the hot and crowded schoolroom at Driel the stench of wet, filthy clothing and bodies was overpowering. Mugs of tea, well laced with rum, were thrust into outstretched hands, but the plates held no more than a minute quantities of the hot stew; it was not that there was any shortage of food, just that the doctors had advised of the danger of overburdening starving stomachs.'

The End of the Evacuation

As the night went on, the Wyvern's engineers, without outboard engines, became exhausted by the repeated crossings and, with more boats being carried further down stream, the size of crews was increased from four to six and eventually to eight men. This, of course, reduced the number of evacuees the assault boats could carry on each trip. As dawn approached, men from 5 Dorset replaced the exhausted Sappers, while 112 Field Regiment fired a smoke screen from 0400 – 0630 hours, as daylight grew. Brigadier Essame recorded details of the operation's closing stages:

'It had been hoped to evacuate the 4 Dorsets after the Airborne Division. Few, however, could be found. As dawn broke the enemy

rained down a murderous fire on the boats, manned for the most part from the Pioneer Platoon of 5 Dorsets; spurts of spray in the Rhine marked where mortar bombs struck the water. The enemy closed in amongst the reeds on the far bank and set up machine guns, which skimmed the surface with deadly effect. Our guns fired smoke to screen the operation but to no avail. Major Vinycomb [206 Field Company RE] *made one last trip in a Storm Boat to the far bank, loaded it with men, and as the enemy drew near made his way back under heavy fire. A young Canadian officer dashed over with two loads of German life jackets and left them on the far shore. Hardly an occupant of his boat was alive or unwounded when he at last reached the home bank. Lieutenant Colonel Henniker, the CRE, had remained throughout the night imperturbable on the riverbank directing the operation. All that could be done was done. To continue in daylight would merely mean useless sacrifice of life. He accordingly ordered ferrying to cease.'*

Having just been posted from 1st Airborne Division, Colonel Henniker must have had an unenviable personal and military decision to make, knowing that former comrades were still waiting on the far bank. The evacuation was halted at 0545 hours.

Altogether, 2,398 soldiers were evacuated from the Oosterbeek Perimeter on the night of 25 / 26 September. Of these 1,741 were from 1st Airborne, 422 were Glider pilots, 160 were Poles, who had either landed by glider north of the river or had crossed on the nights of 23 or 24 September. Only seventy-five Wessex soldiers, out of the three hundred men of 4 Dorset Group who crossed the Rhine the night before, returned. For the second time in just over two months, the Battalion's rifle companies had virtually ceased to exist. Over the coming days, weeks and months several hundred more paratroops and members of 4 Dorset evaded capture and escaped across the Rhine to add to the total of those who survived the Arnhem battle. However, often forgotten in assessing the cost of MARKET GARDEN, is the self-sacrifice of Colonel Henniker's British and Canadian engineers, and the Dorset assault pioneers, who laboured through shell and machine gun fire to evacuate the Airborne Division.

On the northern bank of the Rhine, SS *Hauptsturmführer* Müller recorded his reaction to the dramatic end to the battle, as dawn broke:

'But then it stopped – all of a sudden – the silence appeared treacherous to all and almost "hurt". Was it all over? Would it start again? The Red Devils had withdrawn and disappeared during the night behind the curtain of dirt and destruction.'

CHAPTER SEVEN

ELST – XXX CORP'S HIGH-WATER MARK

While dramatic events were unfolding on the Wessex Division's western flank, following the capture of Oosterhout, there was some hard fighting on the Island's main Nijmegen to Arnhem road. 129 Brigade continued to attack directly up the road but the flat terrain, and embanked roads, was perfect defensive country. Without air superiority and with limited artillery ammunition, progress was slow. However, the Dash to Driel on 22 September had left the German defences in the Elst area open to flanking attacks from the west.

The Germans regarded Elst as the key terrain in their *Sperrverband*, which they formed to contain the threat posed by the arrival of the Poles at Driel. By 23 September, *Oberst* Gerhard's Regimental Headquarters was commanding a mixed bag of troops that included 'infantry' from all three Services, a coastal machine gun battalion and three companies of Dutch-German SS soldiers. However, even if the quality of the infantry was questionable, the original eight tanks that dashed across the Arnhem Bridge to face the Irish Guards, had been reinforced. No less than fifteen brand new Tigers and King Tigers of 506 *Schwere* Panzer Battalion, along with a number of Panthers were now deployed on the Island, along with sixteen 88mm dual purpose guns. Five Tigers were lost to 5 DCLI during the Dash to Driel and other tanks became irrevocably bogged when probing west from Elst. Away from the roads heavy tanks were unsuitable for ground bisected with drainage ditches crossed by weak bridges. Of greater utility, were the ten obsolescent but lighter and more manoeuvrable, *Sturmgeschutz* III from 280 *Sturmgeschutz* Brigade. However, the *Sturmgeschutz* suffered the same disadvantages as the tanks, with the generally short fields of fire in the orchards that surrounded Elst, and in the town itself.

Elst was held by approximately three hundred and fifty veteran *Wehrmacht* infantry of *Kampfgruppe* Knaust, reinforced by infantry from 21 SS Panzer Grenadiers. Another key SS unit deployed to cover the Elst area were two *Nebelwerfer* batteries of SS *Werfer* Detachment 102. These fearsome multi-barrelled 320mm rocket 'mortars', had been withdrawn from the fighting around Oosterbeek to face the threat posed by 43rd Wessex Division's advance to the Rhine.

A Nebelwerfer in action 23 September, near Elst.

23 September – Plans and Congestion

It will be recalled that General Thomas's plan for the seventh day of MARKET GARDEN was to establish a firm grip on the Rhine by passing 130 Brigade Group north to reinforce the Poles and 5 DCLI at Driel. Waiting to follow behind 130 Brigade's column, was 214 Brigade, which was to attack Elst.

With enemy tanks and infantry active between Valburg and Elst, 130 Brigade's move had been slow. Meanwhile, Brigadier Essame's 214 Brigade waited. 1 Worcester, with fourteen tanks of C Squadron, 4th/7th Dragoon Guards, were already in place at Valburg, having followed 5 DCLI the previous evening. However, 7 Som LI, who were to be the second attacking battalion, were stuck, in Oosterhout. At 1300 hours, XXX Corps log records that leading battalions:

> '...have reached final objective in area of river and being shelled from ELST. 1 Worc in VALBURG being counter attacked from ELST and zero for their attack on ELST has been postponed. 130 Bde traffic is still moving.'

As recorded in 4/7 DG's war diary, the Germans to the east of Valburg, who were interfering with 130 Brigade's move, were dealt with by:

> 'C Sqn [who] started at 1200 hrs with the Worcesters. 1300 one Panther reported captured by the Worcesters. 1315 C Sqn reported three Panthers ditched and 1 Tiger brewed up. The ditched panthers were destroyed by us when we came across them. 1400. C Sqn was still

*helping the Worcesters in the village of Lienden immediately west of
ELST. A Sqn still waiting [with 7 Som LI] for the word to go.'*

Predictably, the divisional commander was not happy about the delay.
Brigadier Essame described the problems:

*'Movement by any type of vehicle across the soggy fields was quite
out of the question. Some difficulty was experienced in explaining this
fact to Major General Thomas on the wireless. He accordingly arrived
at the Valburg crossroads to verify the situation in person. Here he
found myself and my commanding officers seated around a billiard
table, settling the final details for the advance on Elst, now at last
feasible. A more than usually vicious concentration of artillery fire,
which smashed all the windows and killed several men outside greeted
his arrival. In the circumstances, his opinion, expressed with his normal
brevity and force, that the rendezvous was ill chosen, must be regarded*

**'Incoming!' British infantry dash to cover before the Nebelwerfer
round falls.**

as fair comment. A second salvo brought the conference to a speedy conclusion.'

Private Bill Edwardes describes the wait for the attack on Elst to begin:

'During the attack on Elst, I was one of two stretcher-bearers attached to D Company. 1 Worcesters were gathered around the Valbourg crossroads, I can't remember where our Regimental Aid Post was but it was normally near Battalion HQ, which was in one of the Orchards by the crossroads itself.

'We had a long day waiting in the rain for the attack to begin. This was not unusual but there was plenty to look at, with 130 Brigade and tanks heading north.'

By mid afternoon, 7 Som LI had reached Valburg but as Brigadier Essame again complained: 'The difficulty of staging a brigade battle with another brigade advancing through your assembly area on the only available road, will be readily appreciated'. However, 4/7 DG's war diary recorded: '1600. Lienden now clear. A Sqn and 7 Som LI commence their attack'.

See map page 112

214 Brigade's plan was to attack with 1 Worcester and C Squadron 4/7 DG, on the left, and with 7 Som LI and A Squadron, on the right. In the first phase they were to sweep patrols and outposts of enemy infantry and tanks from the area between Valburg and Elst that had been tasked by Major Knaust to cut the route to Driel. Having advanced to the area of the De Hoop crossroads, 1 Worcester were to assault Elst, while companies of 7 Som LI were to clear the area to the south between the village and the railway line. This latter move would cut the main highway to Arnhem behind the German positions further to the south.

The Attack on Elst and the Highway – 23 September 44

The first phase of the operation began at 1600 hours. As recorded by Major Watson of 1 Worcester:

'Standing by the Gunner command vehicle... one could hear the word "Fire", a rumble in the distance, the shriek of a shell passing over, and then crash – our artillery were preparing the advance. D Company leading, with tank support, set off down the road passed C Company's location... A crash of 88s greeted their appearance as they debauched into the open country, and small arms spattered from various farm buildings. The tanks replied, the company deployed, and the advance continued. At a bend in the road, a Panther appeared, but its life was very short for it was instantly set on fire by our own tanks, a credit to their alertness... The farmhouses were searched and the enemy found in

**Brigadier Essame and Lieutenant Colonel Osborne-Smith, CO
1 Worcesters, discuss the operations.**

them were quickly disposed of.'

*'Solid shots twanged over head – another Panther appeared and was
engaging our own tanks – darkness descended quickly and we struggled
forward against strong resistance; at last the second Panther that had
been holding us up was destroyed.'*

Private Bill Edwardes was following the Assault Company with his
stretcher:

*'When we got going, I was advancing on foot behind D Company
and we came under artillery fire. The enemy probably had an OP in the
church tower ahead of us. Most of the casualties had multiple shrapnel
wounds and not many blast wounds, which meant that it was air burst
shells, rather than ground burst or mortars.*

*'As we approached, our artillery was pasting Elst and, as we got close
to the village the tanks who were leading, engaged enemy tanks to a
flank. They knocked out two of them; one was a Panther and I think the
other was a Tiger. Our leading platoons got into the village fairly easily.'*

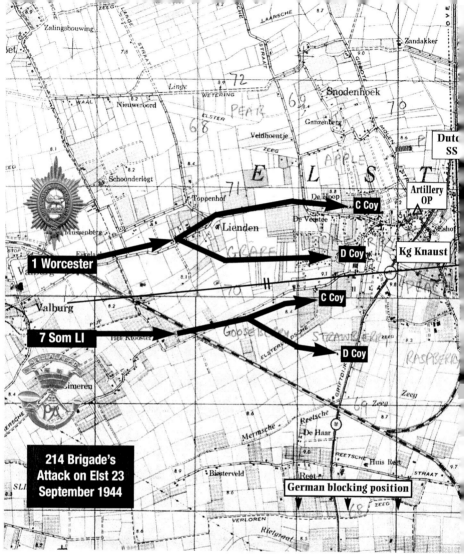

Labels on map:
- Zalingsbouwing
- Zandakker
- Linge
- Nieuwerbord
- Snodenhoek
- Ganzenberg
- Veldhoentje
- Dut SS
- Schoonderlogt
- Toppenhof
- De Hoop
- C Coy
- Artillery OP
- 1 Worcester
- Mussenberg
- Lienden
- De Veestee
- Kg Knaust
- Eikela
- D Coy
- Valburg
- C Coy
- 7 Som LI
- Het Klooster
- D Coy
- imeren
- Zeeg
- Reetsche
- De Haar
- Huis Reet
- **214 Brigade's Attack on Elst 23 September 1944**
- Biesterveld
- Reet
- **German blocking position**
- VERLOREN
- Rietyraal

To the south of the Worcesters, Captain Meradith gives a similar account of 7 Som LI's opening moves: 'The battalion moved off as planned and C Company reached the objective [a crossroads south west of Elst] without serious opposition'. In the second phase of the attack, D Company 7 Som LI took over the lead and continued the advance to the road with A Squadron 4/7 DG in support. 'They pushed on to secure a road junction astride the main road. Meeting slight opposition, they gained their objective just as light failed, taking ten prisoners. The Somersets were eight hundred yards south-west of the town, in a compact lay-out with the battalion right covering the main road running north to Arnhem.' Private Len Stokes, however, recorded that B Company suffered unfortunate casualties:

'We set off in heavy rain and had gone three-quarters of the distance when we were halted by heavy fire from the crossroads. The two company signallers were just behind me. They called for artillery fire but must have made a mistake with the map reference as the 3-inch mortars fell right on us – causing casualties. I was the sole survivor of the HQ Group I was with... After this shambles we had to retreat to our start line and in pouring rain, started the attack again and took the objective.'

The Somerset's attack had succeeded in isolating a *Kampfgruppe* from reinforcement from the north and, at the same time, disrupted German blocking positions between Lent and Elst, which had held 129 Brigade's attacks over the last two days. However, the Somerset's position was exposed and, unusually, according to 4/7 DG's war diary, 'A Sqn stayed out the night with the Som LI on the south side of ELST', rather than withdrawing to an over night leaguer.

The Worcesters were, however, to face an impossible task, having been committed to the time consuming clearance of a village late in the day. Major Watson continued:

'A long straight road gave entrance to Elst, and a tall church steeple in the town itself gave one the feeling (and it was later proved to be correct) that this, as an observation post, gave the Boche a perfect view of our oncoming attack... The outskirts of Elst were reached. It was impossible to undertake house-clearing at night so the Commanding Officer ordered consolidation. C and D Companies took up positions just inside the town on the left and right of the road, A Company lay back in an orchard with Battalion HQ and the Machine Gunners [8

The axis of advance for 1 Worcester was dominated by the church tower at Elst.

Elst Church
tower

Middlesex] *covered the open ground to our left... plans for the final assault the following morning were made by torchlight.'*

The Worcesters, secure amongst the houses, sent the Shermans of C Squadron back to a leaguer with RHQ 4/7 DG near Valburg, as the tanks would have been vulnerable to German tank hunting parties in the dark. The night was, however, 'relatively quiet, except for the occasional burst of fire... and the periodic rumbling of tank tracks'.

To the south of the town 7 Som LI had an interesting night. The battalion historian wrote:

'Now D Company, who had got onto the main road unbeknown to the enemy, were having a good time. Within the next hour the bag consisted of two DRs, one 20mm AA gun complete with crew and towing vehicle, one artillery officer complete with car and one ration truck which was hit by a PIAT. Most of this traffic was going from north to south where the enemy was still holding up 129 Brigade in the area of Reet. However, well after dark, one tank moving in the opposite direction managed to crash past them. At 0330 hours, D Company reported a considerable number of enemy moving north along the road. Artillery fire was brought down, causing a number of casualties but the majority did succeed in getting by and moving into Elst.'

The Second Attack on Elst – 24 September

A message from 43rd Wessex Division to XXX Corps, recorded in its war diary was unusually realistic: '214 Bde are going to have another crack at ELST, in which every house contains a bazooka and a few infantry. Will be a slow job but should be cleared up today.' Shortly afterwards, orders came down the chain of command that artillery ammunition was to be rationed as Hell's Highway had been cut again by the enemy.

Major Watson outlined Lieutenant Colonel Osborne-Smith's intentions for 1 Worcesters on the second day of the attack:

'The plan was as follows: A Company were to swing out into the open country to protect the flanks of B and D Companies who were to do the actual clearing, D Company first and B Company second. C Company were to remain in their present position.

'It was just about to be executed, when the sound of an enemy tank was heard just round the corner before one entered the town proper. Our tank commander decided to see if his own tank could knock it out, and, acting as gunner, he ordered his driver to nose very cautiously round the corner. The tank eased forward, slowly very slowly, then crash – a sheet of flame, and it immediately reversed again. Someone peered

The OP, when in British hands, had to move from the top of the tower due to enemy fire and took up position here

The church at Elst. The tower was used as a German observation post and was burnt out during the fighting.

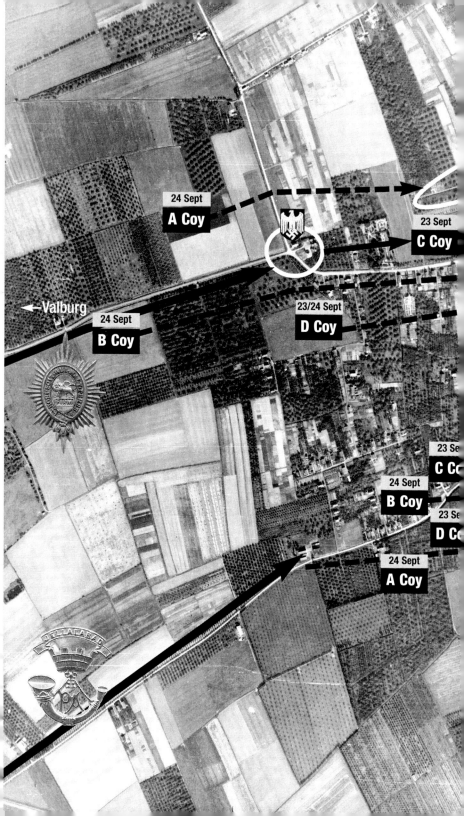

24 Sept
A Coy

23 Sept
C Coy

←Valburg

24 Sept
B Coy

23/24 Sept
D Coy

23 Se
C Co

24 Sept
B Coy

23 Se
D Co

24 Sept
A Coy

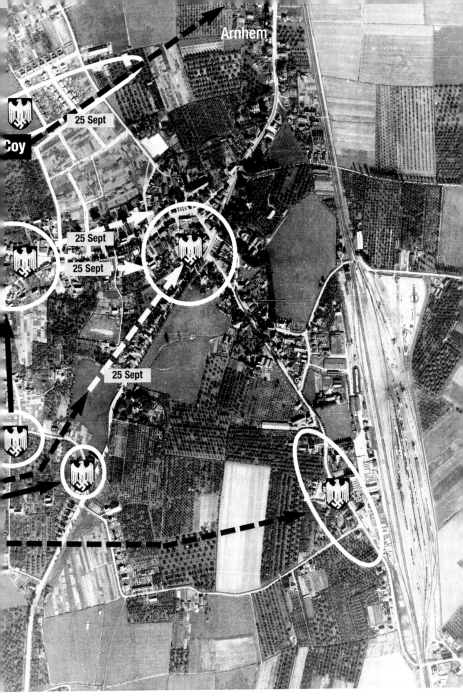

Arnhem

25 Sept

Coy

25 Sept

25 Sept

25 Sept

25 Sept

 German strongpoints

The Battle of Elst 23-25 September. Note the number of orchards surrounding the town.

The interior of Elst Church after the battle. the bullet holes indicate that fighting went on inside the building before it was set on fire by German shellfire.

round the corner and there was the Panther – killed – his turret had been facing the wrong way. On investigation later it was found that this tank, together with others, had come straight from the factory to this front.

'A Company reached their flank position without much trouble and our Mortar Platoon started dropping their bombs in the town.'

As the leading assault company advanced, they came under heavy fire from the houses and it took the personal example of Major Souper to lead the point section forward again:

'They ran from cover to cover, dashing grenades in open windows and trying to destroy the stubborn and heavy resistance, but it was too good to last, whilst running across an open space a burst of fire struck

118

Major Souper, mortally wounding him.'

Stretcher-bearer Private Bill Edwardes was again following the attack:

'This was the first town we had attacked and the training we had done while we were waiting back in Vernon was paying off. We hit the first real resistance in the houses in the outskirts in the form of rifle and machine gun fire and it seemed that every house held enemy infantry. Our tanks followed the Company and blasted hell out of the buildings with their guns and machine guns. Then the infantry went in. In most cases, as our men arrived through the front door the Germans were going out the back and withdrawing to the next building. We had to clear Elst house by house, street by street and it took a long time. Our main concern was the church tower. The tanks put a lot of ammunition into it to drive any Germans up there away but it didn't fall down.

'Some of the German prisoners and wounded were wearing uniforms that I hadn't seen before. I think they were probably sailors or marines.

'In comparison with our previous battles, casualties were not particularly heavy. As the Germans were withdrawing but those who were hit, were got by machine guns on the road. We were following up behind the infantry who were shouting at us and pointing to the casualties. Maybe because the Germans were falling back, we were not fired on (unlike at Vernon) when we went forward to the casualties. This is just as well because we were unarmed, as we left our Sten guns behind because they got in the way when we were trying to treat

A Panther knocked out on the streets of Elst. Notice the gun is facing to the rear. It had been delivered straight from the factory.

Major Knaus the defender of Elst.

casualties. We didn't have far to carry the wounded as the Jeep ambulances were close up behind us. Each time we went back, we would wait for the call for "Stretcher bearers". We would look at each other as much as to say, "Did we hear that?" but we always went forward with the stretcher. We were frightened while we were waiting but fear dropped away when we got busy doing the job. It's afterwards when you get the shakes. The worst part of being a stretcher bearer and a seventeen-year old spotty youth, is that you had to comfort older men and even officers by telling them they were lucky and that they had got a "Blighty" wound, when you knew they were going to die.'

Battalion stretcher-bearers rarely received the recognition or awards that they were due.

Also wounded early in the battle, was SS *Sturmmann* Trapp, who had fought 2 PARA at the Arnhem Bridge and had been sent south with *Kampfgruppe* Knaust, following the Polish drop on 21 September. He recorded that:

'In Elst, I was wounded by small arms fire in the knee. An armoured half track took me back. On board there was also a Wehrmacht major. When I moaned, he showed me his leg and told me to cheer up. He moved painfully on this wooden leg and commanded the battle from a half-track. Later in the hospital in Rees, I discovered that he was Major Knaust.'

D Company 1 Worcester became, as frequently happens in urban fighting, disorganized, as rifle sections fought to clear individual houses and lost touch with their platoon commanders. In addition, as their ammunition ran low and casualties increased, the advance lost momentum. Private Albert Kings recalled how on 24 September, 12 Platoon was only eight men strong, including the platoon commander Lieutenant Fellows MC.

'On the way in, a burst of machine gun fire spat the earth at my feet; the toecap of my boot was shattered and I was bleeding badly. I made my way behind a Sherman tank for cover and then over a road and a fence into the arms of two men of 10 Platoon. Lady-luck had at last deserted me. My war was over.'

B Company, following up behind D, was ordered by Lieutenant Colonel Osborne-Smith to take-over the attack, which proceeded with

Farms on the Nijmegen-Arnhem road in the area of 7 Som LI's road block.

renewed vigour and 'after some very tough hand to hand fighting, cleared most of the town. The Commanding Officer then ordered everyone to consolidate in present positions.' After hours of fighting, daylight was fading and the Worcesters were in no condition to follow up their success and complete the capture of Elst. They had expended virtually all their ammunitions and suffered heavy casualties.

To the south of Elst, having seized a toehold on the Nijmegen – Arnhem road the previous evening, 7 Som LI spent the day consolidating in the area. Their battalion history records that:

> *'At 0730 hours, on 24 September, B Company moved forward supported by one troop of tanks and against slight opposition, occupied another sector of the main road.'*

However, Brigadier Essame, whose HQ 214 Brigade was still located at the heavily shelled Valbourg crossroads, had grander ideas. 'At 0925 hours, ...A Company was instructed to cut across the main road and move due east to the railway line.'

Before the Commanding Officer had given his orders, A Company was attacked by the *Luftwaffe*, who were making the most of the Allied loss of air superiority. Despite this, by 1030 hours A Company with one section of anti-tank guns were in position, having taken two prisoners belonging to the Waffen SS. However, another brigade instruction could not be successfully executed:

> *'At about 1830 hours, orders were received for a company group to occupy the [Elst] station. A Company were ordered to move there but within two hundred yards were held up by enemy machine gun fire. As it was then dark, the Commanding Officer ordered A Company to*

121

return to their original positions and to maintain contact [with the enemy] *by patrols.'*

On 25 September what was to be the day that MARKET GARDEN officially ended, with the evacuation of 1st Airborne Division, 1 Worcester completed the clearance of the north eastern part of Elst. Their historian records:

'The battalion spent most of the day clearing up [the enemy] *and licking its wounds. Visits were paid to the Dutch people who had remained in the town, encouraging them and asking them to leave, but quite a number preferred to remain now that the town was in our hands. Later history relates how they were all evacuated as the town was pounded into rubble and months later flooded by breaching of the dykes.'*

This account makes light of serious opposition still holding buildings in the eastern part of the town. 1 Worcester, had received no reinforcements and little ammunition resupply. Consequently, still located to the south of the town, 7 Som LI's,

See photo page 117

'B Company were ordered to attack and secure the area of the cross roads in the centre of Elst... The Company supported by a troop of tanks moved off at 1000 hours. One platoon moved on the right of the main road and one on the left, through very thick, enclosed, country with many houses and small orchards. One tank which tried to get through this country was immediately ditched and the other two had to move up the main road.

'The platoon on the right was soon held up by machine gun fire across the open ground. The advance on the left of the road, supported by our mortars continued without opposition up to about three hundred yards from the objective. Here it was held up by machine gun fire and snipers at very close range. Just before this, an anti-tank gun in the area of the crossroads had knocked out both remaining tanks. The Company signallers had both become casualties and so the company was out of communication. The Commanding Officer moved forward to discover the situation and finding that the company was pinned down ordered them to withdraw three hundred yards in order to allow artillery fire to be brought down on the enemy. This was done, the artillery fire including 64 Medium Regiment and also the 4.2 and 3-inch mortars was brought down at 1500 hours. The company moved forward and took its objective, and the offending anti-tank gun, without further trouble.

'In the meantime, C Company had moved up west of the town to relieve a Company of the Worcestershires for a further attack. At 1330

The railway line near Elst after the battle.

hours, D Company were ordered to move up to occupy B Company's original position.

'The battalion consolidated in the new positions and the Worcesters came up on their left without further trouble. It was evident that the Germans had decided to abandon Elst.'

5 DCLI, holding the area between Elst and the Rhine saw the remnants of *Kampfgruppe* Knaust and up to ten armoured vehicles streaming north from the town. They engaged them with as much of their ammunition reserves as they could spare to speed them on their way. Typhoon fighter-bombers joined the attack. This was one of the few occasions during MARKET GARDEN when weather and over rigid Allied air space control allowed the Wessex Division air support. German accounts of the battle praise *Oberst* Gehart's officers for rallying the fleeing *Kampfgruppe* north of Elst. They were used to bolster the southern end of the *Sperrverband*, which was held by a weak Dutch-German SS battalion who were now in an exposed position. However, 147 (Essex Yeomanry) Field Regiment RA record in their war diary that they were called upon to switch fire from the Perimeter to an SOS target, on a German counter-attack north east of Elst:

'... which involved a switch of 179 degrees. Fortunately, all the fire orders had been given before the Tannoy box disappeared out of the Command Post, with wires hooked around the tracks of the SPs as they traversed.'

Presumably, 341 Battery's fire mission was successful in breaking up the enemy attack, as none of the infantry war diaries record coming into close contact with a German counter-attack.

XXX Corp's High-water Mark

The battle for Elst was the hardest battle on the Island, within sight of the Arnhem Road Bridge, standing on the horizon just four miles away. However, 2 PARA 's heroic battle had been over for several days and the remains of 1st Airborne Division were evacuated that night, 25/26 September 1944. Despite the ending of Montgomery's great gamble, fighting in the Elst area was far from over. For XXX Corps, MARKET GARDEN, as one platoon commander commented, really 'ended at Elst on the night of 5th October amid smoke and flames like *Gotterdammerung'*.

As a part of General Thomas's reorganization, on 26 September, the Worcesters and 7 Som LI were relieved by 129 Brigade who took over positions facing German positions astride the railway line. 130 Brigade took over responsibility for the banks of the Rhine and 8 Armoured Brigade, reinforced by 43rd Recce Regiment, continued to hold the western flank. 214 Brigade became the divisional reserve.

The badly damaged Elst Church tower was now in British hands, this enabled 129 Brigade's artillery OP to overlook the German positions, but according to 4 Wilts the enemy knew it was being used:

'Forward observation officer of 224 Battery, Captain AJ Townsend, who was in his element – directing the fire of our guns on the Arnhem Bridge and trying to hit vehicles passing over it. Life in the tower was unhealthy; 88mm guns continuously sent solid shot crashing through the masonry, and there were also many attempts to set it on fire with mortar concentrations.'

Eventually, the artillery OP was shelled out of the top of the Elst Church tower and had to take up position lower down.

4 Som LI took over the forward positions in the Elst area. Lieutenant Sydney Jary of 18 Platoon recalls the occupation of defences on the northern outskirts of Elst.

'The Company area was to be on the village side of the main railway line with positions dug into the embankment. Two platoons facing east would hold the embankment and a small level crossing. They were also sited to cover the approaches from the north through the back gardens of houses. The third platoon was to be sited, facing north, astride Main Street in case enemy armour broke through the forward company and came through the village towards Battalion HQ.

'The first day passed without major incident, although we were regularly shelled by some large guns and two self-propelled guns fired airbursts over the junction near Company HQ. We even managed to

heat water in a cottage and the whole company had a bath.

'From the moment of our arrival in Elst, I had a brooding premonition. The quiet few days only accentuated this feeling.

'The enemy decided to make life as unpleasant for us as possible by sudden unpredictable concentrations of artillery right in the middle of our company area. We called them "stonks". One of these shells unfortunately fell, right into one of 16 Platoon's slit trenches. No trace remained of the two men that were in it manning a Bren.

'The once neat gardens and cottages in the Company area were pockmarked by craters and covered with rubble, slates and dust. Cottages collapsed into piles of rubble and the paths and lane became strewn with wreckage. Smiling faces vanished and the grey look returned once more. Men walked with one ear cocked in the air for approaching shells and with a slight stoop. The jokes began to peter out and the cheerful "Good morning, Sir" ceased when I went round the platoons at "stand to". Morale was always higher during an attack. Sitting around being shelled is not an occupation to be recommended.'

Looking west towards Driel from the highway across the Wettering Canal and the railway lines.

Driel

If life was unpleasant for D Company occupying depth positions in Elst, it was about to take a distinct turn for the worst. A Company 4 Som LI had been holding a position north of the village on the banks of the Wettering Canal and had suffered heavy casualties. Lieutenant Jary went forward with the other platoon commanders:

'The whole length of the main Nijmegen – Arnhem road through Elst was under enemy observation. Any movement brought down heavy concentrations of artillery and 88mm airburst. As one got close to A Company, the enemy fired at any sign of movement with increasing ferocity.

'We had hardly gone two hundred yards when hell-on-earth was let loose. A very accurate concentration of 105mm shells burst all around

British Infantry crawl across a gateway that is covered by enemy fire.

The Wettering Canal and the Road to Arnhem. Lieutenant Jary's Platoon position was in the garden and orchard to the left.

us. We rushed further along the road and managed to get out of the shelling. Reaching the railway crossing, we sprinted across and immediately drew 88mm airburst. On the other side was a culvert, three feet deep with water, on the right of the road. We waded in and took cover from the airburst which, by now, was being thickened up by 105s. One 105 shell fell into the culvert behind us, exploding with a deafening roar and sending a tidal wave along the dyke which drenched us.

'Hurling ourselves onto the straw on the barn floor, we lay panting and gasping for breath. John Acock, A Company commander, appeared round the door of the barn. He looked haggard and worn. I doubt if he had slept for a week. The whole Company area was covered by the most intense Spandau *fire and the defensive battle here was one of fire supremacy which the Germans had undoubtedly won. A Company's morale was low.'*

Eventually, D Company had completed the relief in place of A Company in broad daylight, without, miraculously, suffering casualties. Lieutenant Jary continues:

'The Company area was bordered on the left by the main Nijmegen – Arnhem Road. Across the front of the area was an orchard about 250 yards long with a large barn on the right and a house on the left close to the road. Behind this orchard was an open field churned up by shellfire and behind this a large group of farm buildings, dug in around which was company HQ.

'On the second day of our stay in the orchard, Douglas [Gardner] decided to clear the enemy from a few farm buildings that were just across the dyke in front of 16 Platoon's positions on the right of my Platoon. Enemy snipers had crept into them at dawn and caused some casualties. Since they were on his platoon's front, Gordon Bull was to

127

lead the patrol, which was to consist of about six men. At 1400 hours, all preparations having been made and covered by a hail of small arms fire from the whole Company, the patrol rushed across the small bridge in front of the houses. They all reached their objective and, having cleared the house and taken some prisoners, they prepared to return. As they were about to rush back across the bridge, concentrated Spandau *fire came from all directions across the Company's front. It was the most devastating display of small arms firepower that I experienced throughout the campaign. Long bursts of* Spandau *fire tore through the company positions. Branches and slithers of wood from the fruit trees flew in all directions and furrows were torn in the earth, sending grass and soil flying into the air. The parados* [parapet] *of our slit trenches failed to stop this concentrated fire and showers of stones and soil were thrown onto my soldiers crouching below. The Company increased their covering fire but the enemy seemed to have about seven* Spandaus *firing at once. The wretched patrol lay out in the open between the two sides, everyone firing everything they had. One by one, in desperation, the patrol ran from the house to the dyke, jumping into it up to their wastes and wading amidst a hail of fire. They crawled up the banks of the dyke and fell exhausted into the forward slit trenches of 16 Platoon.'*

The junction of the Wettering Canal and the Nijmegen – Arnhem road had taken on many of the characteristics of the 'glory holes' of the Great War, where patrols or movement of any kind was met with an instant reaction. In this area, there was no atmosphere of 'live and let live', as the SS infantry regarded this as the Allied *Schwerepunkt* for a renewed drive to Arnhem. The Wettering Canal, four miles from the Arnhem Bridge was to remain XXX Corp's bitterly contested 'high-water mark' on Hell's Highway well into the winter.

CHAPTER EIGHT

RANDWIJK

The withdrawal of 1st Airborne Division may have marked the end of MARKET GARDEN but for those fighting on the Island, battle was to continue unabated. The positions held by 43rd Wessex Division on the southern bank of the Rhine, became the Allied front line in Holland. These positions were at the end of a sixty mile corridor stretching back to the Joe's Bridge on the Escaut Canal. This corridor, justifiably known as Hell's Highway, was an extremely vulnerable artery and, on the morning of 26 September, it remained cut by *Fallschirmjäger* Regiment 6 and *Kampfgruppe* Jungwirth. Despite the halt in offensive operations, General Horrocks issued a morale boosting order of the day to XXX Corps.

> 'We now stand poised... ready to advance again as soon as our larders have been restocked. I want all ranks to realize that the German is putting up a strong resistance as we approach his frontier. He is however very stretched and provided we can maintain the offensive as we have done in the past, he is bound to crash in time. Very soon we shall be advancing into Germany and carrying on the war on German soil.'

However, there was to be no early renewal of the Allied offensive.

The threat posed by Operation MARKET GARDEN had sucked in German reserves from across Holland and Germany, including, some who had been facing the 1st US Army. By the time Oosterbeek was evacuated, there was a strong German force consisting of the remnants of II SS Panzer *Korps*, elements of 1 SS Panzer, 9 and 116 Panzer Divisions, as well as various infantry and *Volkgrenadier* divisions. Despite the fact that many of these shattered formations were 'divisions' in name only and the *Volksgrenadiers* were of questionable quality, the Germans had been victorious at Arnhem and their morale was high. *Generalfeldmarschall* Model, who had forbidden SS *Brigadeführer* Heinz Harmel to blow the Nijmegen Bridges, now sought to exploit success at

Generalfeldmarschall Model

129

Arnhem and drive the Allies back beyond the River Waal.

It will be recalled that on 26 September, 129 Brigade took over positions facing the railway line to the east, while 130 Brigade took over defence of the Rhine around Driel. To the west, Lieutenant Colonel Fox-Lane's 43 Recce Regiment held the left flank, with a screen reinforced by 12 KRRC, 8 Armoured Brigade's motor battalion, and SP guns of 511 Battery, Essex Yeomanry. 214 Brigade was the Wessex Division's reserve. The front was long and but the sector between Elst and Driel, it was held by observation posts and standing patrols. For example, just three of 43 Recce Regiment's armoured car troops were responsible for almost three miles of the Rhine bank around Randwijk, west of Driel.

The night of 26/27 September was dark and moonless, which favoured *Generalmajor* von Tetau's aim to slip a battalion across the Rhine onto the Island, near Randwijk. At first, the British thought that this bridgehead, south of the Rhine, would be used to mount a major attack. However, a German company commander confirmed that this was a deception and that they had not been aware that the Wessex had deployed so far west. The crossing made at several points, including the ferry site at Renkum, which was used to bring anti-tank guns and other support weapons, went undetected. It was not until 0200 hours that one of A Squadron 43 Recce's 'listening post reported that Germans were digging behind them on our side of the river'. Worse still,

> *'Sergeant Taylor of 2 Troop, manning a Bren gun, was astonished to see in the gloom six Germans hauling an anti-tank gun into position a few yards away from him. He opened fire at once and cut down the whole party... 2 Troop's listening posts had been ordered back to the troop positions which they reached after some confused skirmishing in the dark.'*

The Germans had managed to establish a well supported and coherent bridgehead, consisting of an SS panzer grenadier company and three *Volksgrenadier* infantry companies from *Sich* Regiment 26, under the noses of the British. The fighting began to escalate, as, 'Twenty Germans now approached the troop positions. These were driven off, but confused fighting continued.' Major Scott-Plummer deployed his three troops around the German bridgehead. The recce troops advanced under cover of darkness until they made contact with the enemy. The Wessex's divisional historian recorded that:

> *'At dawn Lieutenant Howe, with Sergeant Carleyon and Sergeant Corless, advanced with three armoured cars and opened fire with deadly*

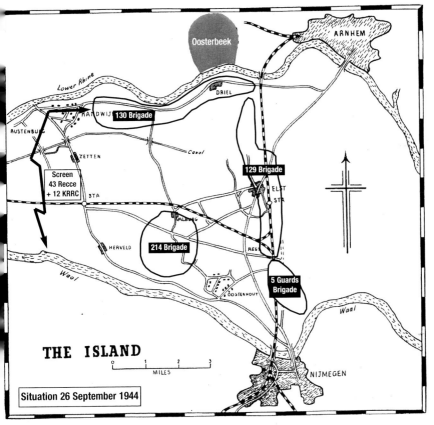

The map shows labels: Oosterbeek, ARNHEM, Lower Rhine, DRIEL, RANDWIJK, 130 Brigade, AUSTENBURG, Canal, ZETTEN, 129 Brigade, Screen 43 Recce + 12 KRRC, STA, ELST STA, VALBURG, 214 Brigade, HEBVELD, REE, 5 Guards Brigade, Waal, OOSTERHOUT, Waal, NIJMEGEN, THE ISLAND, MILES, Situation 26 September 1944

effect on large numbers of the enemy now visible digging in around the dyke. Sergeant Carleton's 2-inch mortar ranged accurately on the enemy's trenches. A violent battle now developed and Panzerfaust bombs and shells began to drop amongst the [British] vehicles.

'... a shell exploded under his car which lurched over the dyke bank and rolled down into a party of Germans. The fate of the crew was unknown... for some time but we were pleased to hear that the three were prisoners.'

The Germans, faced only by the lightly armed 43 Recce Regiment, were able to expand their bridgehead, and occupy a part of Randwijk.

130 Brigade, whose left flank was threatened by the German bridgehead, launched the first counter-attack. 7 Hampshire's reserve company and a troop of 'Shermans, assembled to deliver the attack. 7 Hampshire's war diary records how the battalion had been preparing for another operation when orders came:

'The Orders Group was cancelled and C Company was ordered to

131

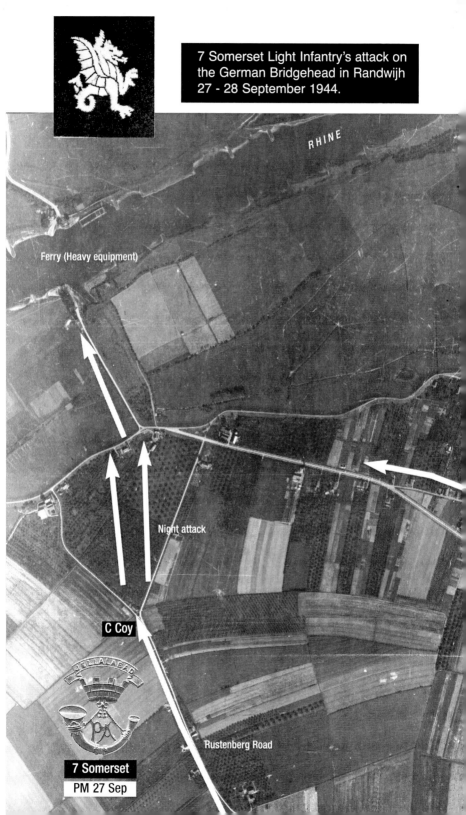

7 Somerset Light Infantry's attack on the German Bridgehead in Randwijh 27 - 28 September 1944.

RHINE

Ferry (Heavy equipment)

Night attack

C Coy

7 Somerset
PM 27 Sep

Rustenberg Road

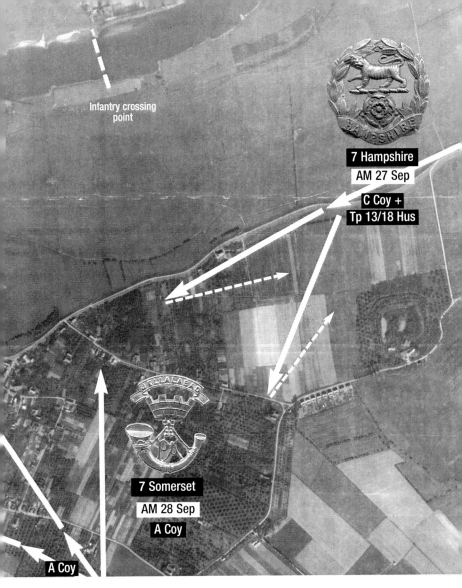

Infantry crossing
point

7 Hampshire
AM 27 Sep

C Coy +
Tp 13/18 Hus

7 Somerset
AM 28 Sep
A Coy

A Coy

*stand-too ready to move. At about 0830 hrs, Recce troops reported
enemy attacking them from the west and C Coy was sent off with one
troop of tanks [13/18 Hussars] to deal with them. The enemy were
encountered near the village of Randwijk just west of Hertern.'*
Lieutenant Colonel Talbot recalled how the Hampshiremen and the
tanks, despite being shelled and mortared, advanced along the dyke
road, pushing the enemy back and:

> *'C Company took up a position in the area of the east road junction*

The open ground and ditch that C Company 7 Somerset used to advance to the Rhine and Randwijk.

> *and engaged them, inflicting many casualties and pushing them back towards the river bank where the enemy turned south. At this time, it was learned that a battalion of 214 Brigade was attacking from the south and in view of this, it was considered unnecessary to reinforce C Company with another Company. C Company therefore established a firm base in the area of the road junction with two sections of D Company occupying the Herten Crossroads.'*

In fact, C Company had done well to drive the enemy into Randwijk. However, in the 'confused and violent' street fighting they became disorganized, in the face of a force over three times their size. Brigadier Prior Palmer of 8 Armoured Brigade, took command of all troops in the area and withdrew the Hampshires to the crossroads at the eastern edge of the village. Accompanying 8 Armoured Brigade were two platoons of 12 KRRC, who along with A Squadron 43 Recce Regiment, established a 'Stop Line' along the Ligne/Wettering Canal. It was obvious that there were insufficient troops to dislodge the enemy *Kampfgruppen*. Therefore, reinforcements from 214 Brigade were summoned. Both 1 Worcester and 7 Som LI were placed on notice to move but only Lieutenant Colonel Borradaile's Somersets actually went forward from their 'comfortable billets'. Mounted on A Squadron 4/7 DG's Shermans, A and C Companies rode to the Stop Line.

While the Somersets were deploying, the artillery was harassing the

134

Germans astride the Rhine. General Horrocks recorded that:

'A member of the Dutch Resistance had come up on the air and reported by wireless that he was in the window of a house at Renkum and could see German troops in considerable numbers crossing the Rhine from north to south. He added that, although he was not a trained artillery observer, he could describe fairly accurately the fall of our artillery concentrations, and this he did with surprising accuracy, causing considerable casualties.'

Meanwhile, arriving at the Ligne/Wettering Canal, Colonel Borradaile's outlined a simple plan. With the support of the divisional artillery, two companies each with a troop of tanks in support, along with their mortar and anti-tank sections, were to advance north towards Randwijk and Rustenberg. Each company group was to use a road as their axis, with C Company on the left and A Company on the right. Both companies debussed at the canal line and deployed into their assault formations, for a late afternoon H-Hour. The Brigade Commander said:

'Ahead for 800 yards stretched completely flat and open marshy fields, in full view of the high ground on the other side of the Rhine. Messeerschmitts swooped down on both columns as they advanced. The fire of 88's made it impossible for tanks to operate beyond the canal.'

Lieutenant Mottrom's 9 Platoon was on the receiving end of the fire from fifteen to twenty enemy aircraft. He said 'Its quite remarkable how troops disappear on such occasions. Ditch or hole leap to the eye - legs propel with piston like urgency - a flying leap, and you wait and hope panting with fear and thrill.'

The infantry advanced with covering fire from the tanks positioned along the Ligne/Wettering Canal and 179 Field Regiment, whose OC, A Company, Major Roberts, said:

'Fired smoke trying bravely to conceal our nakedness. On for another 200 yards when the expected Spandau trilled into life. Down went the section leading on the left of the road, two men wounded. They disengaged and returned the fire, which came from behind a knocked out tank, some three hundred yards to our front. The business of accurately locating and estimating the position and strength of the enemy was brilliantly done.'

Using his No. 38 set Lieutenant Mottrom passed fire control orders to Captain Bridges, the FOO, who directed artillery fire onto the enemy 'with the aplomb of a Salisbury Plain artillery exercise'. However, during the process the 15-cwt truck with the artillery radio aboard was hit by a burst of enemy fire that shattered the windscreen wounding a

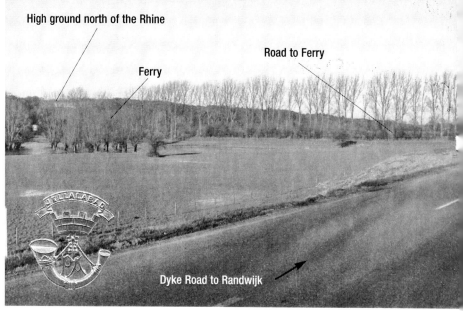

High ground north of the Rhine

Road to Ferry

Ferry

Dyke Road to Randwijk

The scene of C Company 7 Somerset's night attack on Randwijk Ferry.

driver sitting between Captain Bridges and Major Roberts. Realizing that the ditches offered a covered approach, 9 Platoon led A Company to the outskirts of Randwijk but by this time it was dark and as Major Roberts explained:

'I knew nothing of C Company's whereabouts, and my own men were extremely tired, wet and hungry. I therefore decided to make a company strong point some two hundred to three hundred yards from the enemy locality in the shape of a triangle.

'That night, in the pouring rain, we shelled the wretched Germans mercilessly whenever they made the slightest noise. One single mortar bomb would be answered by a troop, battery or the whole regiment. We dished out dinner and held an order-group for a dawn attack.'

Meanwhile, on the left, C Company was attacking in a similar manner down the Rustenburg road. Major Durie wrote:

See photo page 134

'Our route was the usual Dutch scene – ditch and willows on either side of the road, with occasional farmhouses and orchards. The Bosche was well dug in and concealed, and we soon found that the best method of dealing with them was by moving up the wet ditches rather than flanking attacks over very flat ground on either side of the road.'

During the advance, Sergeant Woods of 13 Platoon, led Private Pomeroy forward, who firing his Bren gun from the hip, was instrumental in clearing outlying strong points, killing three enemy

136

and taking twelve prisoners.

Fighting their was across the open ground had been a slow business but by 2030 hours, they were still hundreds of yards short of the dyke road. Major Durie continued:

'We could see the high ground on the opposite side of the river and movement forward had to be very stealthy. The light was beginning to fade and our troop of tanks had orders to return to their forward rally. Owing to the heavy rain and movement along the ditches, the No. 18 set had got damp and ceased to function. I, therefore, decided to consolidate short of an orchard and locate enemy positions in the orchard and on the dyke road, with a view to final attack at first light.'

Just as the Major Durie was siting C Company in all round defence, Lieutenant Colonel Borradaile arrived with orders. In the pouring rain, he explained that 'it was imperative to secure the ferry crossing that night in order to deny the enemy the opportunity of reinforcing his bridgehead'. According to the regimental historian: 'By the light of burning farm buildings a plan was made over rain soaked maps, to put in a night attack to clear the orchard and capture the dyke road'. Captain Meredith explained that:

'The divisional artillery saturated the forward side of the orchard, later lifting to the rear and finally onto the area of the road. The Company took full advantage of his barrage by "leaping on it" so closely that at times the mediums were falling behind us. Apparently, the barrage was to much for the Bosche for we found the many newly dug weapon slits empty. The Company carried out a tight consolidation with great speed and supporting arms were up and in position in less

The Rhine east of Randwijk as it appeared in 1944.

German infantry carrying out a river crossing in inflatable rubber boats at night.

than ten minutes after the objectives were taken. Local patrols went down to the river bank failed to make contact with the enemy but the whole company stood-to at full strength until dawn.'

At dawn, despite their exposed positions on the dyke, C Company dominated the area with the ferry site with fire and patrols.

C Company's night attack had also driven a number of enemy away from the western part of the bridgehead into Randwijk, where A Company were awaiting dawn to renew their attack. The CO approved their plan and promised Major Roberts that he would be supported by the divisional artillery. Before dawn, a patrol was sent out to confirm that the enemy was still in position, as they had become 'quiescent, probably through our shelling'. However, on approaching the enemy position they opened fire, confirming that they were still active.

Captain Meredith wrote about A Company's final assault on the German bridgehead with just seventy men:

'At 0600 hours the attacking Platoons, 8 and 9, went forward from their overnight positions, supported by a divisional concentration and the three-inch mortars to keep the village of Randwijk quiet, and, more closely, by 7 Platoon who thickened the covering fire with guns moving along the flanks of the attacking troops. The attack was a huge success mainly owing to the tremendous weight of artillery. The enemy in their slits in the wood must have experienced a foretaste of hell, for several slits had direct and many Germans were totally dazed. We took more than our own numbers in prisoners alone, and forged forward to link up with C Company who were now on the river at the ferry. The battle was

not quite over, however, for some SS who had evaded our mopping up and waylaid our transport as it came up with ammunition. A lively battle was waged by the drivers, and the SS finally escaped into the village. Randwijk was later mopped up after a gun duel around the church.'

The enemy bridgehead was destroyed and A Company alone took one hundred and thirty prisoners on the morning of 28 September.

The Second German Crossing

On 1 October 1944, *Feldmarschall* Model ordered a general attack on the extended XXX Corps front that stretched from the Groesbeek Heights, via Nijmegen and the Island to the Rhine. With the considerable resources that had been directed to stopping MARKET GARDEN, Model now felt that he could drive the vulnerable Allies back from the Reich's borders. One part of the attack was an assault across the Rhine in the Radnwijk area, which was still held by 7 Hampshire.

The troops allocated to this task by *Generalmajor* von Tettau, were SS *Hauptsturmführer* Oelker's battalion from Lippert's SS NCO School Arnheim. In the days following 1st Airborne's drop, this battalion had been expanded and around a core of experienced SS soldiers, with the attachment of companies of military artisans, *Kriegsmarine*, recruits from Herman Göring Training Regiment and a company of ordinary *Luftwaffe* personnel. Oelker's battalion fought throughout the battle on the western flank of the Oosterbeek Perimeter. However, after the evacuation, SS *Hauptsturmführer* Oelker recalls that he was instructed:

An SS unit crossing a river in rubber boats.

Second Army artillery continued in support of 43rd Wessex Division on the Island.

> '...to form a bridgehead south of Arnhem over the Rhine, and hold until a defence line north of the river had been established. Strong British force were to be pinned down at the same time to achieve this aim. "The bridgehead is to be secured and held no matter what the cost" – so read the order!'

In fact, the crossing was a deception measure, designed to attract 43rd Wessex Division's attention from II SS Panzer *Korps's* main attack on the eastern flank. A measure of the Oelker's success is given by the fact that 69 Brigade complained that it only belatedly received the divisional artillery support it needed to hold the German's main attack at Bemmel (see Chapter 9). See map page 147

The crossing was to be made astride the ferry site at Kastle Doerweth just over a mile downstream from the Driel ferry. SS *Hauptsturmführer* Oelker recalled that,

> '*Preparations continued night and day. Immense problems became apparent; there were no assault pioneers or heavy weapons. At H-hour, 0600, division had supplied only four boats; where was the army supplement?*'

He went on to say:

> '*The first wave crossed over with frightful casualties. Our own artillery did not fire enough. I watched this bizarre attempt at an attack whereby some SS men were only able to reach the far bank by swimming and were then immediately engaged in hand-to-hand combat on arrival.*'

Following behind the SS Company was SS *Hauptsturmführer* Oelker's headquarters in an assault boat with a failed engine:

> '*We paddled. A brave* Heer *engineer NCO stayed in the rear of the boat, directing our efforts otherwise we would have drifted off course. He was instantly killed by a shot through the chest. As we neared the bank, a machine gun burst hit the boat, injuring two men and puncturing it. I was lucky the burst only grazed my knee. The boat drifted away with our two comrades lying in it. I never saw them again. We lay on the muddy bank the entire day, and nobody would go forward.*'

Lieutenant Colonel Talbot, Commanding Officer 7 Hampshire, records the attack from the British perspective:

> '*The enemy attempted to force a crossing, under cover of a thick morning mist and heavy mortar and artillery fire on the whole battalion's position. The enemy were at once engaged by our own artillery, mortars, MMGs and LMGs but despite heavy casualties, a number succeeded in establishing themselves on the river bank.*'

River Rhine

Flood Plain

The Brick Factory occured by Oelker's **Kampfgruppe** opposite Kastle Doerweth.

After a day with its forward companies pinned down on the riverbank, the remainder of *Kampfgruppe* Oelker was still on the Kastle Doerweth bank. However, under cover of darkness SS *Hauptsturmführer* Oelker led his battalion forward from their bridgehead to attack the brick works two hundred and fifty yards across the flood plain. He recalled: 'We attacked the objective from the right, something the British had not anticipated. But where were the rest of the troops? Where was the signals detachment?'

Throughout the following day, 7 Hampshire sought to deal with the incursion into their area. The CO recorded that:

'B Company and later C Company counter-attacked but in spite of several gallant attempts with good fire support, they were repeatedly held up by heavy MG fire and accurate mortaring. They did, however, succeed in containing the enemy to a small area. During the next night the enemy made further attempts to reinforce but several of his boats were sunk or damaged by our defensive fire.'

Amongst those crossing that night was the *Luftwaffe* Herman Goering Training Company, who were ordered forward for a crossing after dark. Herbert Kessler was with them:

'In the evening, it got livelier. We were ordered across the river. We marched to Kastle Doerwerth and at midnight I received orders to cross. The pioneers and rubber assault boats are supposed to be already on the bank, ready for us. We move forward. We can't find any pioneers and the boats are all shot to pieces. Then up comes a messenger from the rear. "No crossing! The moon's too bright!"'

Colonel Talbot wrote about operations on 2 October:

'At Dawn C Company, with one platoon of A Company under command, made another effort to deal with the enemy but were once again held up. At mid-day, under cover of smoke, the enemy once more reinforced their bridgehead and again suffered heavily in doing so.'

Again, Kessler had been sent down to the river.

'We got the order: "Cross at once!" My group was the second to *move forward. The first group carrying two rubber dinghies went towards the bank. One dinghy was immediately shot to pieces, the group leader was severely wounded. Those 200 metres to the bank were under heavy artillery fire as well as flanking fire from machine guns. I received orders for my group to try it. I jumped up, together with my platoon, run to the boat, which is still intact, tear down to the water,*

SS troops repeatedly attempted to emulate the American 82nd Airborne at Nijmegen — a river crossing under fire and in broad daylight.

jump into it with three other men, and row it across the river. This all sounds so harmless, but I shall never forget that rowing. The shots splashed into the water all around us like hailstones, and how did we manage to get to the other side, I don't know. Still under fire, we dug our holes. That crossing in bright daylight was nonsense.'

The reinforcements that trickled across the river were barely enough to keep up with casualties, as the British pounded away at the German bridgehead. The final group, the *Luftwaffe* Company, did not cross until the night of 3/4 October. Having crossed Kessler described life in the bridgehead:

'One didn't dare get out of the hole, for any reason. I think there were now about twenty of us left, with only one machine gun.'

The Hampshires continued their attacks on Oelker's bridgehead:

'That night A Company put in an attack which penetrated the factory buildings but unfortunately a heavy river mist rose, visibility was reduced to about one yard and was pulled back until visibility had improved. The Company attempted to push forward again at dawn on 3 Oct but surprise was lost and it was held up and had to be withdrawn back across the open fields under cover of smoke. During the rest of the day the factory was "softened up" by field and medium artillery.'

It is no wonder that SS *Standarten-Oberjunker* Lindemann reported that his commanding officer expostulated 'This bridgehead is absolutely senseless – we should give it up'.

During the following days *Kampfgruppen* Oelker could hear the sounds of battle to the east where 10th SS Panzer Division (see Chapter 10) was probing across the railway lines. A day later, a determined attack was mounted by 363 *Volksgrenadier* Division on the Allied flank at Opheusden, four miles to the west. However, neither German attacks managed to link up with the German bridgehead in the Brick Factory. On 10 October SS *Hauptsturmführer* Oelker finally ordered the abandonment of the lodgement after continuous counter-attacks, shelling and scant resupply.

A British infantry section moving in Holland.

CHAPTER NINE

THE BATTLE OF AAM – BEMMEL

By October 1944, the British Army had been at war for five long years. On campaign for most of that period in the desert, Sicily, Italy and brought back to spearhead the invasion of Europe, was the 50th Northumbrian Division. Consequently, the men serving in that division had seen more than their fair share of fighting. Such had been the infantry casualties since D-Day that the British Second Army had run out of infantry replacements and to keep divisions up to strength others had to be broken up. Controversially, 50th Northumbrian Division was considered by some to be a 'non-fighting division', the soldiers of which 'spent too much time looking over their shoulders'. Despite replacement of key commanders and the incorporation of the fresher 231 Infantry Brigade, the Division's overall performance was

still considered to be below par. The Battle of Aam-Bemmel was to be their last battle and one that was to be as difficult as any of their previous engagements.

In the days following the ending of MARKET GARDEN, 69 Brigade, under command of 43rd Wessex, was holding positions facing east, against *Frundsberg's* increasingly determined attempts to recapture the Nijmegen Road Bridge. SS *Brigadeführer* Heinz Harmel was under pressure from *Feldmarschall* Model not only to capture the bridge for future operations but also to remove the Allied bridgehead from the Island.

XXX Corps intelligence officers warned of impending attacks and on 30 September, the first blow fell on a narrow front against 5 East Yorkshire Regiment (5 E York) at Bemmel. This attack, in daylight, across open

Feldmarschall Model and SS **Brigadeführer** Harmel.

145

ground was stopped by machine gun and artillery fire.

On 1 October, *Kampfgrupe Frundsberg* mounted a powerful attack on the Island across the Wettering Canal. This attack, however, was only a small part of the overall German offensive that fell on XXX Corps' front. The enemy *Schwerepunkt* on the Island was Bemmel, held by 69 Brigade guarding the most direct approach to the Nijmegen Bridges. Captain Mason of 7 Green Howard, recalled how, using the intuition of an experienced soldier:

> *'The acting adjutant had a premonition that was that something was going to happen. On his own initiative, he stood the battalion to at 4 a.m. It was a good thing he did, because at 5 a.m. they attacked. They came in with everything they had. ... Practically all the rifles were smashed to bits by shell fragments because the men had left them on the trench parapets.'*

The enemy 'loomed up through early morning mist, and were soon within fifty yards of the forward companies'.

7 Green Howard's forward positions were pushed back by SS infantry and panzers, who followed close behind their creeping barrage of mortars and artillery. The Yorkshiremen had been assured that there was little German armour on the Island, so it came as a surprise to see panzers making their way into the heart of their defences, avoiding their company positions. C Company was forced back, 'exposing A Company, which was left in an isolated position'. However, by 0700 hours, the German advance had been held but for the remainder of the day, the Yorkshiremen and SS soldiers were locked in close combat; neither side prepared to yield ground.

The regimental historian recalls how Private Edemenson helped break up a renewed panzer attack at about 1030 hours:

> *'One Tiger came across the open field by Heuval Farm, where it got within seventy yards of No 11 Platoon. After firing five PIAT bombs, he brought it to a halt. One German got out, and waving his hand, shouted in broken English, "You win this time", and ran off as hard as he could'. The remainder of the crew were 'accounted for.'*

However, 124 Field Regiment's historian recalls that, in the general attack on the Allied positions:

> *'It soon became apparent that the main attack was directed on the 69 Brigade front but in the early stages 43 Divisional artillery was employed on their front, and 55 and 124 Field Regiments had to support*

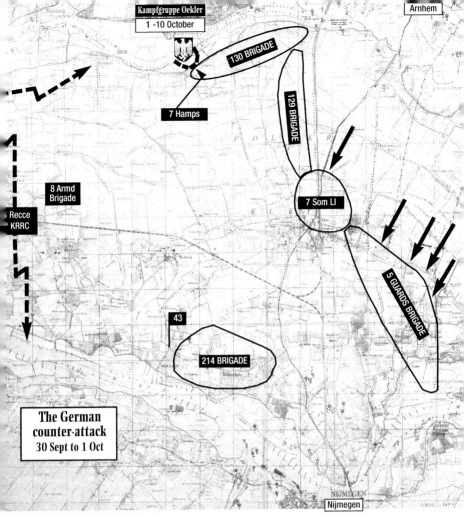

5 Guards Brigade and 69 Brigade. The regiment [124] was
continuously firing DFs and when not engaged on 69 Brigade front
answered calls from 43 Division.

'12 enemy tanks sent against 7 Green Howards, and although two
were knocked out the remainder succeeded in infiltrating between B and
C Companies. This forced C Company to give ground, and exposed A
Company, who were soon isolated.

'During this period, our OPs continually engaged enemy tanks and
infantry, causing heavy damage and casualties to the enemy. A
favourite concentration area of the enemy was an orchard; this became
a Regimental target, and the "directing staff" lost count of the number
of times this target was engaged both by the Regiment and by 43

147

Division artillery. Their additional fire was provided when badly needed on our Brigade front at critical times.'

The Brigade and unit war diaries highlight two figure from the day's logistic SITREP relating to the fire support given to 7 Green Howard. During 1 October, 124 Field Regiment alone fired 12,500 rounds of 25-pounder HE, while the medium machine guns of B Company 2 Cheshire fired no less than 95,000 rounds of .303 ammunition. Clearly, with Hell's Highway secure, there was no longer a serious concern about ammunition.

As the German attack was taking place all along the Allied lines, there were few reserves immediately available to reinforce threatened points. Consequently, it was not until 1800 hours that 5 E Yorks, with a squadron of 13/18 Hussars, were tasked to restore the position and relieve 7 Green Howard. However, at 2300 hours when the relief was completed, after eighteen hours in action, Sergeant Hearst said, 7 Green Howards were 'cut up pretty bad, with shrapnel and machine gun fire and had lots of casualties'.

In order to thicken up the defences and enable the depleted and exhausted Yorkshiremen to regroup on 2 October, 151 and 231 Brigades relieved 69 Brigade. These brigades took over positions in an arc from the Arnhem – Nijmegen road to Bemmel. With the situation restored and with a favourable force ratio on his eastern flank, General Horrock's thoughts turned from holding his positions to improving his defences. Therefore, 50th Division was given a limited mission to secure a tactically advantageous position. 1 Dorset's war diary described the detailed aim of the attack, which was to take place on 4 October:

'This is the result of the Corps Comd's decision to make our position secure by driving the enemy back to the line of the Wettering Canal and recover the ground lost in recent enemy counter-attacks'.

By recapturing the Wettering Canal, 50th Division could hold German attacks at a decent distance from the Nijmegen Bridge.

Plans and Objectives

50th Division's plan, in three phases, was for 231 Brigade to capture the orchards northeast of Bemmel. This was to be followed by an attack by 151 Brigade, which was to take the hamlets of Baal and Haalderen. The third phase, also to be carried out by 151 Brigade, was the clearance of two factories on the banks of the Waal.

Brigadier Stanier's plan given to 231 Brigade's O Group at 1400 hours on 3 October was for an attack by 1 Dorset on the left and 1 Hampshire on the right. Each battalion was to be supported by a

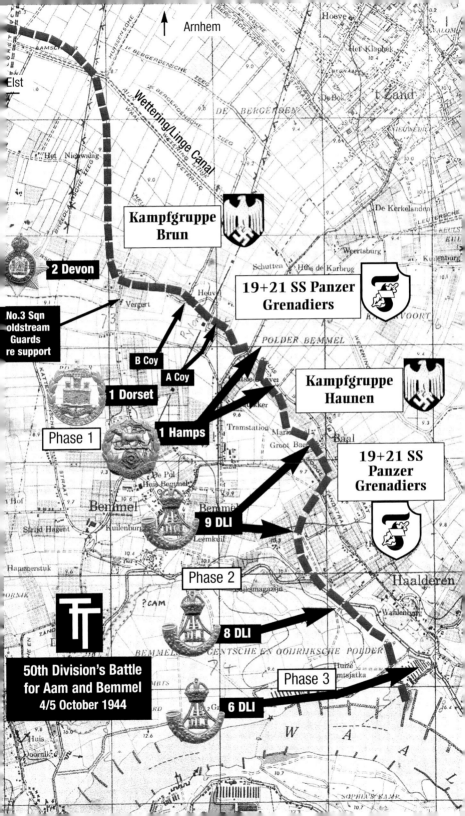

Arnhem

Elst

Wettering/Linge Canal

Kampfgruppe Brun

2 Devon

No.3 Sqn oldstream Guards re support

19+21 SS Panzer Grenadiers

B Coy

A Coy

1 Dorset

Kampfgruppe Haunen

1 Hamps

Phase 1

9 DLI

19+21 SS Panzer Grenadiers

Phase 2

Bemmel

Haalderen

8 DLI

Phase 3

50th Division's Battle for Aam and Bemmel 4/5 October 1944

6 DLI

Squadron of Sherman tanks from 1 Coldstream Guards, the divisional artillery, 2 Cheshire's medium machine guns and heavy mortars, as well as M10s (3-inch guns) from the Corps Anti-Tank Regiment. Overnight, patrols were to have a detailed look at the ground. H-Hour was to be at 1200 hours the following day, 4 October.

In Phase 2, which was to begin, at 1400 hours, two hours after the initial assault, 151 Brigade was to attack from its positions on the outskirts of Bemmel with 9 Durham Light Infantry on the left and 8 DLI on the right. The following morning, the operation was to be concluded by an attack on the two riverside factory areas on 151 Brigades right flank.

A paragraph from 50th Division's Intelligence Summary No 86, describes the enemy facing 50th Division:

'... PWs taken have confirmed what was thought to be the enemy's policy: mixed battle groups composed of stragglers from all units under the sun and of drafts from various training establishments, both Army and Air Force, have been left to hold the front line, while the Panzer Grenadiers of 9 SS Pz Div and of 10 SS Pz Div, forming, as they do, more homogeneous bodies capable of concerted and co-ordinated action, are held in reserve to carry out the necessary counter-attacks.

'Nominally, the troops opposing us amount to roughly eight battle groups of Battalion size, although a few of them are probably weaker. Battle Group Brun is in the sector NW of Heuval.'

Phase 1 – 231 Brigades attack on Heuvel and the Orchards

As ordered, patrols had been sent out overnight to familiarize commanders with the ground over which they were to attack and to identify enemy positions in detail. However, owing to the open nature of the ground little additional information was gained to flesh out the operational orders. Following confirmatory orders, at 1030 hours the following day, the companies started the short move to their assembly areas. Recalling the ground over which he had to lead his battalion, Lieutenant Colonel Bredin wrote:

'The ground was absolutely flat, intersected by many deep ditches, which prevented movement off the roads for wheels and tracks. The orchards and ditches gave good cover to the defenders, while the large pieces of open ground in front of their positions had to be crossed by the attacking troops.'

As planned, the attack began at 1200 hours, under cover of 4.2" mortar and medium machine gun fire. Across the Brigade front, the enemy replied with their artillery defensive fire tasks. On the left, supporting

The White Barn and Orchard which were B Company 1 Dorsets' objective.

Coldstream Guards fire support

Pylon line

Heuval

1 Dorset, Number 3 Squadron, 1 Coldstream Guards' tanks engaged targets from a firebase established in 2 Devon's area, around the hamlet of Vergert. The Dorset's A and B Companies, astride the pylon line, steadily fought their way forward. However, at 1300 hours the Battalion log recorded that enemy fire on 1 Dorset was taking a toll. 'C Coy in assembly area (near Tac HQ) suffers several casualties from enemy shell fire and Major Thomas OC C Company is killed.'

Lieutenant Colonel Bredin commented that 'It was the heaviest shelling we had encountered since Normandy. Very soon, as our leading troops emerged from the orchards onto the open ground, the enemy *Spandaus* opened up'.

The Battalion's post action report recorded that having reorganized in D Company 1 Hampshire's position, A Company assault across the open ground on the right:

> '8 Pl was disposed to deal with some enemy MG fire from the right flank. 7 Pl and 9 Pl, with the Company Commander well to the fore, charged across the open with great dash and into the enemy position. 7 Pl attacked and killed six Germans in a strongpoint based on a building and both platoons overran the enemy positions.'

Word, at 1330 hours, from the forward companies that the Battalion's initial objectives had been taken, was accompanied by the news that another company commander had fallen. Major Harris was killed and that 'Both companies have suffered considerable casualties'. The war diary goes on to say that 'There is still considerable mopping-up to be done and very stout resistance is being encountered'. However, during the mopping up the flush of success led to a certain loss of control. As described in the Battalions report, 'Touch was lost with 9 Platoon, which was later found to have advanced beyond its objective, loosing heavily.' Consequently 8 Platoon 'was brought up on the right to help mop up the orchard and a couple of farm buildings in depth.' This platoon also dealt with enemy dug-in in a 'younger extension of the orchard' not shown on the maps immediately to the north. Meanwhile, 7 Platoon dealt with enemy positions firing out to the north, enfilading B Company's attack on Heuval. Seven Platoon was reduced to just seven men but Sergeant Collins and his men had already contributed significantly to the success of the attack. Sergeant Collins was awarded the DCM for his part in the battle. A group of SS soldiers trying their tactic that had been used so successfully in Normandy, of letting the leading assault troops pass before 'coming to life' and attacking following waves, was dealt with by Company Sergeant Major Elgie. For this and his support to his Company Commander, Major Laugher (who earned an MC), he was awarded the Military Medal.

As the roads and tracks in the battle area were known to be mined, following up close behind A Company were the Battalion's assault pioneers opening the routes forward. It was important to be able to bring up support elements, particularly anti-tank guns and artillery observers, whose presence would be necessary to beat off the inevitable SS counter-attack. Once clear of mines, one troop of Coldstream

Guards' tanks were able to join A Company and assist with building clearance.

Meanwhile, B Company on the battalion's left, with the objective of Heuval, as recorded by Lieutenant Colonel Bredin:

Captain J D O'Neill RAMC, 1 Dorset's doctor alongside his ambulance Jeep, used during the Battle of Aam.

> '... had made as much use as possible of ditches in the initial stages of their advance, but eventually they had even more open ground than A Company to cross. 12 Pl right and 11 Platoon left reached the objective with great dash across the open.'

The two platoons gained a foothold in the enemy position to the south-east of Heuval but were unable to overcome the enemy in the hamlet built on a patch of slightly elevated ground. With out effective communication with Battalion Headquarters and supporting arms, 10 Platoon was then passed through to assault the Company's next objective, an orchard one hundred and fifty yards further on to the north-west.

> 'The Company had to carry out a considerable amount of mopping

A Company HQ, 1 Dorset, taken between Heuval and Bemmel.
Left to right: Sergeants Martin and Turner; Lieutenant Boorman; CSM Elgie MM; and Captain Dartnell.

up in the ditches, which surrounded the orchard, and which afforded such good concealment for the enemy. As soon as they realizes we were in possession of the orchards and Heuval, the Germans put down heavy concentrations on our new positions.'

While reorganizing his company to consolidate his hold on the objective and complete the clearance of Heuval, Major Harris had to stand up to make himself heard and to give hand signals to his platoons. In doing so, he was killed by a shell splinter. Captain Luff, the Company Second in Command took some time to make his way from main B Company HQ forward and

The CO, having heard nothing from B Company over the radio, had a company runner, dispatched by Major Harris at 1245 hours, wounded in front of him before he could fully deliver his message. Lieutenant Colonel Bredin dispatched a platoon from D Company to help 'clear up the situation there'. He went on to say:

'But the position at Heuval was not really secure, and as B Company had suffered heavily, the Commanding Officer ordered the advance to Heuval of the whole of D Company, who were getting well stonked where they were. The task given to them was to complete the mopping up of the area and, with B Company, to make it into a strong point. Finally, if occupying the orchards north of Heuval was a practical proposition. [The enemy withdrew and the orchards became no-man's-land].

'During this advance the enemy to the north of the Devons' right

A member of B Company 1 Dorset fires his sten gun into a building during the clearance of Heuval.

A carrier belonging to 2 Cheshire knocked out while bringing medium machine guns forward to the 'White Barn' at Heuval.

locality at Vergert [Kampfgruppe *Brun*], *brought considerable enfilading* Spandau *fire to bear on D Company's leading platoon. To get the company into Heuval I ordered the tanks to advance north from Vergert* [with 17 Platoon] *to neutralize the enfilading* spandaus. *Meanwhile D Company covered the "dangerous space" in double quick time!'*

The arrival of D Company enabled the last SS soldiers in the area to be killed or captured. It was not long before reports were passing up the chain of command confirming that the enemy were from 19 SS Panzer Grenadiers (9 SS Panzer Division) and 21 SS Panzer Grenadiers (10 SS Panzer Division), grouped in SS *Brigadeführer* Heinz Harmel's *Kampfgruppe Frundsberg*.

Happy that the situation at Heuval was under control, the Commanding Officer moved to the right flank, where he found the 'Young Orchard' to be a problem. Occupying it would have exposed A Company far more than envisaged, so a section of the carrier platoon was called up along with a 'man packed' section of medium machine guns from 11 Platoon, C Company 2 Cheshire. At 1630 hours, with the Assault Pioneers having cleared the routes forward of mines, the

Battalion's anti tank guns were brought up.

The Battalion's midnight summary recorded that forty Germans had been killed at A Company's objective and thirty at Heuval and that they had 'a bag of nearly a hundred, mainly SS, PWs'. However, the Dorsets had suffered eighty-nine casualties during the battle. The divisional historian recorded that *Kampfgruppe* Brun,

> '... *suffered very heavily and lost two complete, as the remnants of 5 and 8 Companies, amounting to roughly 30 men surrendered to us this evening in the orchard. Its present strength is probably now little more than 100 men.'*

1 Hampshire's Attack

50th Division's Intelligence Summary No. 86 describes one of the *kampfgruppen* facing 1 Hampshire south of Heuval: 'Astride the road at 743690 was Battle Gp Hauen, a small unit of approximately 60 men consisting of stragglers of all descriptions'. However, SS *Brigadeführer* Harmel had positioned less reliable troops, such as Hauen's in strong positions, with key terrain being firmly held by his SS panzer grenadiers.

Attacking at the same time as 1 Dorset, the Hampshires assaulted the German positions located south-east of Heuval, with the support of Number 2 Squadron 1 Coldstream Guards. Major Wright's A Company led the Battalion's attack, with the tanks standing back giving fire support. However, as the Hampshire's regimental historian described:

> 'The battle of Bemmel was a bitter and bloody day's fighting, with

A Forward Observation Officer's carrier from 90th Field Regiment knocked out near Heuval Farm.

the SS troops resisting fiercely in every dyke and orchard, and their artillery and mortars bringing down heavy defensive fire. Casualties to the 1st Battalion were unfortunately heavy.'

The enemy mortar and artillery fire was particularly effective during this battle. The fragile valve technology radio sets of the day did not stand up to rough treatment in wet drainage ditches. Also with radio operators pressing them selves into the merest fold in the ground other manpacked sets were hit by shell splinters. Both Lieutenant Colonel Turner's Tactical HQ and the Battalion's main CP were badly effected as, 'The enemy's fire was so heavy that every vehicle at the Battalion Command Post was riddled with shrapnel'. The CO was forced to attempt to command using the radios in one of the tanks, while Major Drewitt the 2IC, at Alternative Battalion HQ, took command of the battle routine and the Battalion's rear link to HQ 231 Brigade.

As is often the case, the fight became a battle of wills and the determination of junior commanders. One such was Sergeant Medway who was:

'... commanding the left-hand platoon. He hated Germans and he had been killing them on every possible occasion since the first encountered them in Sicily; he was a most aggressive fighter who had seen as much action as anyone in the Battalion.'

Sergeant Medway earned the MM for his determined leadership of his young platoon. Major Wright, of A Company received a Bar to his MC for his part in leading the attack but was wounded later, when a shell landed by his slit trench. Amongst those killed during the reorganization phase on the captured enemy position, was Sergeant Slade MM. According to Private Rex Long,

'He was moving around us, redistributing our remaining ammunition and pointing out our arcs of fire when he was hit.'

Casualties were particularly high amongst junior commanders, with five subalterns wounded and one killed. Perhaps more serious was the loss of experienced Senior NCOs, such as Sergeant Slade. Altogether the attack cost the Hampshires sixty casualties.

The above account only makes slight reference to the part played by Numbers 2 and 3 Squadrons, 1 Coldstream Guards. It will be recalled that the ground was too soft for armour to deploy off the roads and the Germans has liberally sown the area infantry of their defensive positions with anti-tank mines. However, the Shermans from fire positions were able to suppress the enemy with their main armament and coaxial machine guns. Suffering the same Guards'restrictions on movement German tanks were kept at bay by the 17-pounder Sherman Fireflies. Brigadier Stanier, himself late of the Welsh Guards, thanked the Coldstream Guards for their support to 231 Brigade. Referring to the reports of his two commanding officers he wrote:

'The success of the attack was very largely due to the whole hearted support given by the Coldstream Guards, who imbued the infantry with great fighting spirit'.

Having lost their positions to the Dorsets and the Hampshires the SS soldiers were left without credible defensive positions south-west of the Wettering Canal started to withdraw suffering further casualties.

Phase 2 – 151 Brigade's attack on Haarlderen

Two battalions of the Durham Light Infantry (DLI) mounted their attack at 1400 hours. 8 and 9 DLIs' mission was to take the hamlet of Baal and the village of Haarlderen, gaining observation over the flat ground beyond, thus driving the remaining Germans east of the Wettering Canal. The regimental historian recorded:

See map page 149

'Shortly before the DLI battalions commenced the advance, news came through that attack by 231 Brigade was going well. Promptly at 2 pm the 8th Battalion moved forward in extended order over ground which had been cultivated in small plots, and through numerous orchards. There was the deafening roar of low-flying aircraft as RAF Typhoons swooped down to attack the German defensive positions with rocket fire.'

8 DLI's initial advance went well with A Company following up closely behind the artillery barrage. However, against varying quality of defenders, some attackers had greater difficulties than others. C Company, who had lost many experienced men in Normandy, advanced slowly and the SS, who emerged from their foxholes as the barrage moved onto depth positions, pined them down. The enemy had made skilful use of the dykes, ditches and orchards and managed to hold up the leading platoons.

'Lieutenant Morrison, with the reserve platoon, was ordered to outflank the Germans while the rest of the company contained the enemy fire' and the young soldiers of C Company fought through the enemy position. D Company was brought up from reserve to take over from C Company and was soon advancing, without the benefit of

158

artillery support as the fire plan had taken moved on well ahead of them. By 1730 hours, Haarlderen was taken and all objectives had been reached, sixty prisoners had been captured, and the old hands reckoned it had been one of the easiest attacks the Battalion had ever had to carry out.'

In addition to the prisoners, twenty German bodies were recovered for burial from the enemy positions. The Durhams suffered forty casualties.

See map page 149

9 DLI, advancing on a two company frontage, had similar experiences, with their C Company also being halted by Germans who survived the barrage. Their accompanying FOO halted the artillery fire plan and re-engaged the German position. C Company cleared the enemy positions and resumed the advance. On the Battalion's right flank, D Company had made excellent progress and within half an hour they had cleared intermediate objective and were heading towards Baal.

'As the advance made headway, German resistance stiffened and A Company encountered some heavy Spandau fire and lost all its officers save Captain Thomas, the second in command. But despite these setbacks all the Battalion's objectives had been taken by 4 pm and in addition to a hundred prisoners the booty included some nine anti-tank guns, mortars bazookas and two half-track vehicles.'

The initial hard fought battle by 231 Brigade had clearly 'unhinged the German positions' and 151 Brigade benefited. By the time the third phase of the operation was mounted, the following morning, 6 DLI secured the area of the factories on the banks of the Waal with ease, against opposition that largely melted away before their advance.

SS *Brigadführer* Harmel wrote of 50th Division's attack on the Aam – Bemmel line:

'The 4th October was one of the costliest days the 10th SS had suffered since the fighting in Holland started. The vitals of the Division had been torn out to such an extent that it was not capable of offensive action in the immediate ensuing period.'

Given that the *Frundsberg* had been fighting in Nijmegen and on the Island since 17 September, against three of the finest Allied divisions, this is praise indeed for the Dorsets, the Hampshiremen and the Durhams. This was a fine end for a famous Division that was shortly broken up to provide reinforcements for other divisions and to make available men with operational experience for the training organization back in England.

160

CHAPTER TEN

THE SCREAMING EAGLES ON THE ISLAND

In October 1944, in order to clear the Schelt Estuary and open the port of Antwerp, the British Second Army needed additional divisions. Use of the intact port facilities was vital to the Allied cause, as it would shorten the lines of communication, which still stretched back to Normandy. Consequently, it was an uncontroversial decision for an American division to remain under command of the British. The, 101st US Airborne Division's paratroopers, trained as shock troops, found themselves in the unfamiliar role of static defence along ten miles of the Rhine between Elst and Opheusden.

Following their epic battle on Hell's Highway, some twenty miles south of the Island, 101st Airborne Division had been expecting, as the divisional historian recorded, 'to be relieved within seventy-two hours. It actually took seventy-two days.' Exhausted from ten days of marching and counter marching to keep the Germans away from Hell's Highway, the American paratroopers moved to the Island.

After two weeks of fighting on the Island, 43 Wessex Division was to be pulled back into positions around Nijmegen, where it was to refit and be XXX Corps's reserve. The relief-in-place began on 4 October with the arrival of the 101st Airborne's tactical headquarters and recce parties that initially set up alongside their British counterparts. The actual front line relief-in-place happened on the nights of 4 to 6 October. Due to the exposed nature of the positions, some of the Wessex's anti-tank guns, mortars and artillery were to be left behind and relieved in slow time. The Sherman tanks of the Scots Greys (4th Armoured Brigade) and the infantrymen of 5 DCLI, who had been the Wessex Division's reserve, were also to remain on the Island under command of the 101st. Lieutenant Colonel George Taylor, commanding 5 DCLI, recalls that General Horrocks thought that to be attached to 101st Airborne 'is a great honour'. However:

> 'A great honour it might have been, but I could only reflect ruefully at the time that "bang goes four days rest out of the line!" As the

American General's mobile reserve, we set up headquarters in a railway station near Andelst.'

The Relief-in-Place

The relief was difficult throughout the divisional area but no where was it more difficult than in the sector held by 5 Dorset near the railway. The Germans were one side of the railway embankment and the dyke, with the Dorsets in close proximity the other side. In addition, the Germans held a farm building, which formed a salient into the Allied position. C Company were in a most exposed position, with German patrols slipping across the railway to their south as darkness fell. 1st Battalion 501 Parachute Infantry Regiment (1/501 PIR) were to take over from 5 Dorset. US First Lieutenant Frank Fitter, along with his Commanding Officer and the Adjutant, were to take over battalion headquarters:

'I remember when we moved up to relieve the British near Driel. As communications officer, I was in the advance party... just as we got there, they were under a pretty heavy artillery barrage. We jumped out of our jeep and ran into their headquarters, which was in a house that was all sandbagged. They had a bunch of noisy radios – had fire control on one side and the CP group on the other. The commander [Lieutenant Colonel Coad] welcomed us in the ole British tradition with: "We're in a bit of a battle now but would you chaps care for a toddy of rum?" We told him, "No, go on with your business." But he insisted, so we drank".'

5 Dorset's history records that,

'... some of the officers arrived during the day to make arrangements for the take over which started about 1700 hours... A Company which was in reserve near Battalion Headquarters sent out several fighting patrols to located these parties and deal with them. One of these patrols under Lieutenant Dyne, linked up with the American company which was to relieve C Company and together they fought their way through the Germans and reached C Company about midnight.'

Taking a southerly route, Company C 1/501 PIR, moving east along the track from Driel, fought through Germans who had earlier crossed the railway embankment. Enemy machine gun fire was soon supplemented by mortar fire. T/5 Carpenter wrote:

'It hit right at the junction of the roads just like it was zeroed in. Then they started dropping the shells towards the north, one after another, each one closer than the others right up the road. The darned things were literally hitting the road and our guys were lying off the

162

*side of the road on each side. We were pinned down... It was the one time
I was ready to break in the entire war.'*

Moving off the road 'The Germans in the farmhouse fired a flare.
Everybody who was moving in the field froze... It was like an eternity
before the flare went out. We took off running across the field and then
infiltrated our way into the British area.' Staff Sergeant White, however,
described the move as being '...every man for himself to get out of the
orchard and into our area'. The relief was eventually completed, with
American paratroopers occupying the British positions under fire. C
Company 5 Dorset then had to exfiltrate out of the area, avoiding the
dangerous track and Driel. At 0330 hours the Dorset's duty
watchkeeper, sitting in the back of a carrier recorded in the Signal Log
that 'all companies are clear of the area'.

The Americans had hardly settled in to their positions, when at
dawn, as recorded by T/5 Carpenter:

*'The Germans started coming in on us from the north. They were
shooting at us and throwing hand grenades over the dyke and we were
throwing grenades the other way. There wasn't much going on up on
the railroad but the Germans were trying to stick their heads through
that underpass and taking some shots. This went on all day.'*

The Dorsets had been having problems with the underpass. They knew
that the 116th Panzer Division had brought up two *Sturmgushutz* that
fired through the underpass at anything that moved on the Dyke Road.
However, the vehicles had remained the other side of the railway

**The barn and ruined farmhouse used by 5 Dorset and 1 Bn 501
Parachute Infantry Regiment, 101st Airborne Division, for their
battalion HQ.**

embankment but in case of attack, the Dorsets had laid a 6-pounder anti-tank gun to fire on the underpass. Meanwhile, Company A was attacking the enemy located in the farmhouse and sensing that they were about to lose this important position the Germans sent the *Sturmgushutz* through the viaduct. T/5 Carpenter recorded:

> 'The British sergeant was urging his men to get to the gun. They said something to the effect that a mortar round had blown the sight off and they wouldn't move out of the farm, which was pretty substantial. He was yelling at them that the tanks were coming – one tank had breached the underpass opening and started shooting at us – all the guns in Company C were firing. I was standing outside that little farm and looked down and saw the gun. I had never fired one of them, never seen one before, nor been close to one. I grabbed another guy and said, "Come on, let's see if we can make that gun work!" I darted about five yards and jumped in the hole they had dug. I didn't know if it was loaded. I fooled around, pulling all kinds of leavers and finally got the breach open. Out popped a shell. It was loaded... While working all the levers, I hit something that caused the gun to go off. The gun jumped in the air. There was a helluva lot of smoke and flame... The shell had hit the tank... The other tank reversed and backed out of the way.'

Amongst the casualties during the relief-in-place was Major General Maxwell D Taylor, commander of the 101st. Further West the General arrived at an OP overlooking the Rhine and the German positions beyond. Captain Karabinos wrote:

> 'We got into the OP and climbed to the top floor and through the peepholes we looked across the river. The General turned to one of the boys and said, "Private, how about directing one of our mortar sections to drop a few rounds across the river." The private replied, "If I were you, sir, I wouldn't do that." General: "Why not?" Private: "Well sir, we have no target of opportunity to fire at, and if we shoot over there, the Jerries will only fire back at us." General: "Fire away soldier, we want to see what goes on over there." So with that, the private picked up his telephone and called his mortar section, gave them co-ordinates

A panorama looking across the area that 1st 501 PIR took over from 5 Dorset.

Driel   Farm held by Germans

Germans north of Dyke Road

Highground north of the Rhine

The underpass in the railway embankment. Inset: the StuG knocked out on 5 October.

The knocked-out Sturmgeschütz positioned on the west side of the underpass.

rm

Anti-tank gun

Rhine

Dyke Road

Underpass

German infantry far side of railway embankment

Farm

Rhine

Germans positions

Driel Dyke Road

The Dyke Road positions after the Germans had been driven out. Blown bridge in background.

Gerald Higgins

of their targets and told them to fire six rounds... After watching six rounds [with no discernible effect], *the General told the private that was enough and with that we proceeded to climb down out of the OP... It wasn't long after that we heard a gun go off from across the river and the whistling of a shell as it came down and hit the other side of the dyke knocking mud across the top and splattering us. Of course, we had a good cover so no harm done.*

'Again, we heard the same gun go off but this shell landed 25 yards to our left. We started double-timing for cover. The gun went off again and this time the whistling sound seemed to be right on top of us. I found myself being hurled some five feet through the air... The General was picking himself off the ground and said "The sonsabitches got me in the ass!"

Also wounded in the arm by shell splinters, General Taylor spent ten days in hospital, presumably lying on his front, having earned a Purple Heart. Brigadier General Gerald Higgins, the Assistant Divisional Commander, took over control of the coming battle.

166

Knocked-out Sturmgeschutz

Inset: The underpass today.

The Battle of Opheusden

506 PIR moved on to the Island during the evening of 4 October. By 2100 hours, they had taken over the western flank, with 3/506 PIR holding the ground between the Rhine and the Waal, which was three miles wide at Opheusden. The 101st's historian describes the ground:

> 'Breaking up the flat expanse was a two-track railroad running east and west whose embankment rose more than five feet above the surrounding land. North of the railroad was the main drainage canal of the Island [the Ligne/Wettering Canal]. Opheusden, a small town of about one hundred brick buildings, lay between the Rhine and the railroad. It could be approached from the east by two roads, one along the dyke and the other running between the railroad and the drainage ditch. Just east of the town, the latter ran into a north-south road, which bridged the ditch and crossed the tracks near a small station. As was to be expected the hills north of the river gave the Germans excellent observation on both roads.'

Facing the Americans was 363rd *Volksgrenadier* Division, reformed with young, infirm or ageing men, following its mauling in Normandy. Its

167

presence had been detected by the British but their strength and mission, to clear the Island from the west, had been missed. Their build up had been slow, as they had to ferry the division across on to the Island by rubber boat and their limited heavy equipment by local ferries.

3/506 PIR, deployed in a light screen, were attacked at dawn. This was the beginning of a three-day battle. The Regiment's after action report recorded:

> *'At 0600 hours* [5 October] *enemy attacking in strength along entire 3rd Battalion front. 3rd Battalion reports enemy using civilians as a screen for their advance. Medium artillery shelling of combat team command post at 0700 hours ...The enemy continues to press his attack and 3rd Battalion commits its reserve at 0845 hours.'*

Elderly, infirm, and youngsters in their early teens, were beginning to make their appearance among the German units. More often than not they were cheaply kitted out.

The first probing attacks, which set off the newly laid trip flares, were held, as the Germans had been unable to accurately locate the British positions and were further confused by adjustments the Americans made during the relief-in-place. Nonetheless, Company G in Opheusden suffered casualties. T5 Edward Vetych, the Company Runner, recalls:

> *'The German attack on our front found me at the company CP, a schoolhouse near the centre of town as the artillery hit with a roar at the crack of dawn. I had taken off my boots for the first time since coming to Holland.*
>
> *'The whole roof and part of one wall were blown in. I was in my sleeping bag and was pretty well buried under debris. ... There were yells for "Medic!" everywhere.'*

Amongst those hit in the first salvos that struck the CP, was Company G's commander Captain Joe Doughty. T5 Edward Vetych continued:

> *'The Main Line of Resistance was in a drainage ditch along an apple orchard on the edge of town. As I got to Lt Rowe's CP, the Germans were in the orchard directly in front and so close I could see the black boots through the branches. Everyone was firing continuously... As I talked to Lt Rowe, he suddenly pulled his .45 and reached out of the window and shot straight down. I glanced back out the door and a*

The Opheusden School in ruins after the battle. Company G's CP.

German soldier lurched out beside the building, with blood gushing from his mouth. Lt Rowe had shot him through the back of the neck.

'About this time a German machine gun got a line of fire down the drainage ditch and 2nd Platoon started taking casualties and had to drop back to the building at the edge of town.'

As the fog dispersed, the Allied artillery came into action and, loosing momentum, the *Volksgrenadiers* fell back. With a better idea of the 101st's positions, Germans artillery replied. Consequently, the 363rd Division's second attack prospered well, with a company attempting to cross the Rhine to join SS *Hauptsturmführer* Oelker's positions at the Brick Factory drawing away reserves. Lieutenant Andros, a platoon commander in Company H, recorded:

Colonel Sink

'When the attack started, it got pretty heavy with quite a bit of mortar and artillery fire coming in. It must have been around 0830-0900 in the morning. We were suffering a lot of casualties, so I sent Swanson back to bring up some litter bearers.

'About 0930, Colonel Bob Sink arrived and he asked me "What the hell is going on?" I told me were getting our butts kicked. So he said, "Can you hold on for another half hour? The 1st Battalion is coming up and they'll counter-attack through you." All I said was "Yeah, we can hang on for half an hour." But I think we stayed on about an hour and a half.

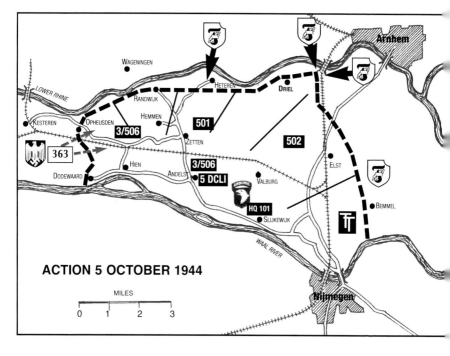

ACTION 5 OCTOBER 1944

MILES

0 1 2 3

> *'When the Germans started getting behind the railroad embankment... Sgt Hefner took his 60mm mortar tube without base plate and put it on the ground and I said I'd spot for him. He stripped all incremental charges off the mortar shells and the first dammed thing went straight up and I saw it coming down. It landed about ten yards from us. But after that Hefner just dropped those rounds right along the back of that embankment. You could hear those Germans yelling. It must have been pretty effective.'*

Second Lieutenant Stroud's platoon of Company H, holding the area of the road / railway crossing, was faring better in stronger positions.

> *'We were pretty well protected, except those fellows on the left who had to be in the fields. I had my CP in the little concrete signal station. We, at one time, had a few Germans trying to surrender, waving a flag. We were holding fire, when a British Bren gun carrier came up and deliberately fired into them killing most – the rest went back.'*

Moving around his Battalion's area, directing operations and stiffening their morale, Major Oliver Horton was killed by shrapnel near Opheusden railway station. The loss of this fine commander at a crucial moment in the battle was tragic. Lt Stroud was there:

> *'A little later, our battalion commander came up to look over the situation and saw where our platoon was placed. We went out about a hundred yards in front of our lines between a couple of houses to try to*

spot the Germans and were mortared. I got up but Major Horton didn't. I turned him over and saw he was white and bubbling at the mouth. I pulled him back as far as I could but he was pretty well gone.'

The regimental reserve, 1/506 PIR, was located at the Andelst-Zetten Railway Station some four miles behind the front line. During the first attack at dawn Colonel Sink had reduced their notice to move. At 0900 hours two companies were ordered forward, supported by Shermans of A Squadron 4th/7th Dragoon Guards (4/7 DG), to reinforce 3/506 PIR. The third company remained as regimental reserve, due to a threat from across the

Major Horton

Rhine. Company A led the advance, under German artillery fire, along the railway line with a troop of Shermans. Two platoons and a troop of tanks reinforced Company H, who were able to hold the vital road/railway crossing. Meanwhile, the third platoon cut north to reinforce Company G in Opheusden. Company B, supported by the remainder of A Squadron's tanks, dug in behind the forward companies to give depth to the hitherto, thin American defences and prepared to mount counter-attacks. 5 DCLI was ordered up from the 101st's divisional reserve and was allocated to Colonel Sink as his new regimental reserve.

The reinforced 3/506 PIR held the attack and the Germans fell back. However, respite for the Paratroopers was no to last long, as early in the afternoon the enemy mounted a third attack, this time supported by armour. However, 3/506 PIR had not only been reinforced by infantry and tanks but also by artillery forward observation officers (FOOs). The guns of 321 Glider Field Artillery Battalion and the British 179 Field Regiment Royal Artillery were now in direct support, with the guns of XXX Corps's artillery also available. Despite the artillery fire, the German infantry, using the cover of drainage ditches, closed in on Company G in Opheusden. The medical officer of 3/506, Captain Ryan, recalled:

'By late afternoon of October 5th, the German had taken most of the town of Opheusden and had the aid station surrounded. German soldiers in the attack could be seen all around and unescorted German wounded came in for treatment... Pandemonium reigned in Opheusden that day and evening, the town was burning and shells were landing

everywhere. One was as likely to encounter a German as an American. All the wounded [79 of them] were finally evacuated by midnight, 3rd Battalion having been relieved by 1st Battalion.'

The German attack was contained in Opheusden by determined infantry combat and artillery fire. 321/GFA and 179 Field Regiment both fired approximately 1,500 rounds during 5 October. Repeated costly attacks had sapped the German's morale and, consequently, future attacks lacked the levels of commitment shown earlier in the battle.

The Germans sensing that there was to be no breakout at Opheusden, late in the afternoon, mounted a fresh attack further south, spearheaded by assault guns. This time they attacked Company I, on 3/506 PIR's, who had only been subjected to relatively light probing attacks. Although they were thinly spread, Company I held the frontal attack but they were unable to prevent a German flanking move along the banks of the Waal. Fortunately, 17-pounder guns of 59 Anti-Tank Regiment, left behind by 43rd Wessex Division, were positioned in this area and held the panzers until a troop of Sherman tanks from A Squadron 4/7 DG arrived. British artillery and tanks with the American paratroopers, in what the divisional historian describes as a 'desperate attack, later restored the lines'.

As darkness fell, Colonel Sink sought to reorganize his front. 1st and 3rd Battalions were mixed together and had suffered casualties that had reduced their combat effectiveness. With the arrival of 5 DCLI as his reserve, Company C 1/506 PIR was available for use in the line. His plan was for all three companies of 1/506 to be positioned around Opheusden, while to the south, 3/506 would hold positions astride the railway line and south to the Waal. The Germans, however, continued their attacks under cover of darkness and during a period when the two battalions were moving to their new positions seized an important piece of ground. The divisional historian recorded:

'As Company H pulled back to readjust its line, the Germans were lucky enough to use the opportunity to move down the railroad tracks into the area around the tiny railroad station, where the road crosses the tracks.'

A 4/7 DG Sherman belonging to the troop left behind in the area of the rail crossing was knocked out in the darkness by a German anti-tank gun, when their supporting infantry cover moved away. Extremely vulnerable in the dark, the remainder of the troop pulled back, keeping the enemy under fire. This penetration of the Allied positions was serious, as not only had it formed a salient into the defences but also denied the tanks, who could only move any distance by road, an important manoeuvre option.

On 5 October, having failed to assemble sufficient combat power for decisive action, 363rd Division's attacks had gained some ground before being held by the numerically inferior but qualitatively superior American paratroopers. The German *Volksgrenadiers* were ordered to mount further attacks and the following day, they brought up fresh reinforcements with which to resume operations. Meanwhile, Allied commanders had a sleepless night as they made plans to recapture the rail crossing and retain control of Opheusden.

Opheusden – the Second Day

Fighting resumed at dawn on 6 October, with both sides advancing along the railway. 957 *Volksgrenadier* Regiment was advancing east, with a battalion either side of the tracks, seeking to exploit the success of the previous evening. Coming the other way was Company G of 3/506 PIR, supported by a troop of British tanks, with the limited aim of recapturing the rail crossing. The result was a numerically unequal but ferociously fought meeting engagement in open country.

A simultaneous German attack was mounted to the north of the railway line, with infantry assault, supported by *Sturmgushutz*, on 1/506 PIR's Company A in Opheusden. Corporal David Patton of Company B, having spent two fruitless hours patrolling the town's south-western outskirts during the early part of the night, wrote:

'At daybreak, it was extremely foggy and I got out of my foxhole and looked around, and suddenly, in a break in the fog, we saw a complete semi-circle of German tanks lined up to the west at about one hundred meters approaching our orchard positions at a slow, deliberate speed. Soon I saw more tanks along the road and on the railroad tracks to the direct south of our position. Sgt King and I hollered at our first line of men to retreat and get out of there for we had only a couple of grenade launchers, three bazookas and light machine guns.

The vital railway crossing taken by the Germans on the night of 5/6 October, thus denying its use to Allied tanks.

The Battle of Opheusden 6 October 1944

At the point where the Rhine and the Waal are only three miles apart the village of Opheusden was of considerable tactical importance.

Dyke Road

DAWN

Opheusden

Church

1/506

5 DCLI

Mill

657 Volkesgrenadier Regiment

1/506

Railway

Posi Mid 6

DAWN position 6 Oct

Ligne/Wettering Canal

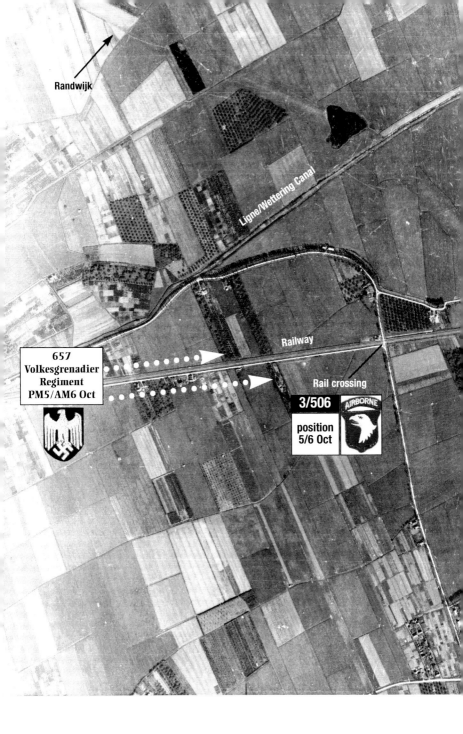

Randwijk

Ligne/Wettering Canal

Railway

657 Volkesgrenadier Regiment PM5/AM6 Oct

Rail crossing

3/506

AIRBORNE

position 5/6 Oct

'There appeared to be hundreds of tanks – though I would venture that 50 were coming at us from three directions.'

Staff Sergeant Mitchell, also of Company B, wrote 'Daybreak came and so did the Krauts! Out of the morning mist the tanks came with supporting infantry directly into the left flank of 3rd Platoon.' 3rd Platoon withdrew further into Opheusden Corporal Weise was soon engaged by tank fire and was joined in his foxhole by a dud German 75mm shell:

'I left my hole immediately. We received word to withdraw and had every 1st Squad man tactically withdraw one at a time. As soon as the last man left, I started to withdraw but heard an incoming shell that hit very close. Shrapnel entered my back causing paralysis.'

Sergeant John Boitano of 81 Anti-Aircraft / Anti-Tank Battalion and his Squad of .50 cal machine gunners, had not been told of the withdrawal and:

'...looked around and there were no infantry around anywhere. Daylight or a little after, a British tank came up beside us. The tank commander stuck his head out of the hatch and said, "We've got word the Germans are going to attack through this area. They've got quite a few armoured vehicles and a helluva lot of infantry."

'Just about then a streak of fire came zipping across his bow. He was right. There was a bunch of tanks out there in the little wood off to our right and one of them was trying to get him. He just stopped in midword and backed out of the line of fire.

'One hundred and fifty yards straight ahead, it looked as if the German Army was doing close order drill. They were coming from two different directions into a drainage ditch. This was a machine gunner's dream. I hit the triggers and nothing happened. It had a broken firing pin. There were three of us and three thousand of them. The decision was made!'

The whole of 1/506 PIR was soon pushed back. At the eastern edge of Opheusden, Sergeant Mitchell shouted 'Lets get into the buildings and make a stand there because we can't fight tanks in the open.' The German attack ground to a halt. However, Colonel Sink could see that 1/506 PIR would not be able hold another attacked. He stressed the importance of holding current positions until 5 DCLI moved up on their left flank. Colonel Sink outlined his counter-attack plan:

'1st Bn. On the right, 5th DCLI on the left, with he main east-west street of Opheusden as the boundary. The attack was to proceed through the town of Opheusden to the western edge and deny the enemy the use of the town.'

176

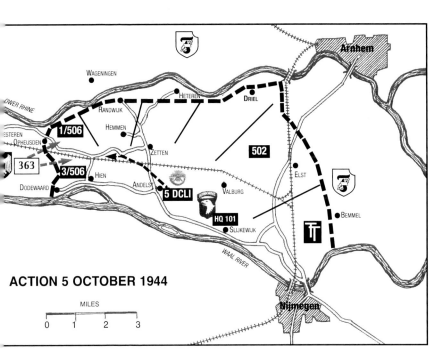

ACTION 5 OCTOBER 1944

MILES

0   1   2   3

Lieutenant Colonel George Taylor, Commanding Officer 5 DCLI, recalled:

'The information was somewhat vague, but it appeared that a group of US troops were holding out in the area of the mill, while others, supported by tanks of the Scots Greys, were guarding the road and railway area a couple of hundred yards east of the bridge.

'The Americans had very little artillery of their own and our gunners were engaged in hostilities elsewhere... The attack, with the DCLI on the left and the Americans on the right, was to be supported by a very thin barrage of mortar fire... Colonel Sink stressed that speed was vital, although I managed to gain an extra 30 minutes for preparation. The attack was fixed for 90 minutes from completion of the conference. I gave out my orders. There was a confident air about our men as I briefly outlined the plan to B and C Companies, assembling in an orchard near the US command post. But it was apparent to us that this feeling was not shared by all the Americans.

'Brigadier General McAuliffe, the tough American hero of Bastogne, had sat in with us while I was giving out my orders. I sensed that he was not quite sure of his 'Limy' allies. On the other hand, Brigadier Essame [214 Brigade], who arrived at the end of the order group, was clearly worried what might happen to his DCLI, owing to the lack of artillery support.

177

General McAuliffe

'Guided by an American officer who knew the ground, D Company set off along a ditch that ran alongside the road, out of sight of any observers in the south side of the village. They left the protection of the ditch and moved north across the first footbridge over the dyke and through a copse. They came under heavy German artillery fire and the advance became somewhat disorganized. With his men delayed, [Major] Spencer finally pushed on with less than half the company. He reached the area of the mill and made contact with a US Major who had 150 men under his command.'

The counter-attack was due to start at 1230 hours but as Colonel Sink explained: 'Because of numerous delays, the attack did not begin until 1345, following a 15 minute artillery preparation.' One of these delays was due to Major Spencer's need to regroup his badly dispersed company. George Taylor continued his account of D Company's attack.

'On a whistle signal from the Americans, both forces swept forward. The Germans waited for them to cover the first fifty yards before opening fire with six light machine guns from a ditch about 80 yards from the road. But their aim was wild, and D Company's two leading platoons led by Sergeant Baron and Lieutenant Snell, surged forward firing from the hip and hurling grenades. The machine gunners were all killed or captured, and the Cornishmen swept on, knocking out two more posts. It was then that the enemy brought in their 88s and mortars.

'Sergeant Baron and Private Smithson fell dead only a few yards from the hedge. Another stout hearted man defying the withering fire, set up his PIAT [a spring propelled type of bazooka] and knocked out a machine gun behind the hedge.'

The Allies had brushed aside the German outposts despite artillery and HE rounds from the supporting *Sturmgushutz* and advanced three hundred yards but the DCLI came up against the enemy's main position, sited in depth along a hedgerow.

Sergeant Brininstool of Company A 1/506 PIR, remembers the last minute co-ordination:

'The English arrived with about 300 men. They said, "You take the houses [along the east-west road] and we will take the open ground to our left flank." We were doing a good job of clearing out the houses but the battle didn't last too long as the Germans mowed the English down.'

An American corporal also saw D Company 5 DCLI in action:

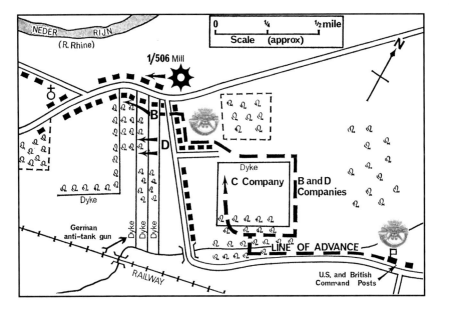

'I remember watching a British unit attack across some fields. They just lined up and away they went. About 25 yards later, only three or four of them were still running... Another British platoon came in, lined up, started running – same thing happened.'

This platoon was under Lieutenant Durden's command. With his own casualties, his company commander and Lieutenant Snell both wounded, all he could do was to consolidate gains and beat off a counter-attack, using three captured *Spandaus*. The wounded were evacuated to the mill. 'It was to the Germans' credit that they observed the rules of war and did not fire while this was going on.' Lieutenant Colonel Taylor continued: 'Eventually, Major Hingston, with just one B Company platoon arrived at the mill area, which was full of British and American wounded.' The German artillery barrage was effectively sealing off Opheusden from significant reinforcement. The wounded Captain Spencer advised Major Hingston that he should attack south of the road towards the church. 'It seemed sound enough advice, and the Americans, despite their tiredness and losses, were game to try again [with Company B].' Having eventually gathered the scattered B Company 5 DCLI together, as Colonel Taylor observed from the mill:

'The combined attack started at 1600 hours. The first 200 yards of B Company's thrust was unopposed and 10 Platoon and Company HQ were able to establish themselves in a big house.

'While awaiting a signal from the Americans, three Germans strolled up. Two were speedily dealt with. A third was seen slipping away and in a short time the company found itself the subject of a heavy

179

mortar attack, which took a steady toll.

'Then the combined Allied assault began in earnest. With the American commander on the right giving the order, B Company surged forward to an elevated piece of high ground beyond the Orchard. Two sections of 10 Platoon were badly mauled as they tried to work their way through the Orchard. The rest of the Platoon moved through the gardens of a row of detached houses.

'They went cautiously from house to house, towards a big building at the end that would give them a good vantagepoint over the enemy. As our men reached it, the house was hit by a mortar shell and burst into flames, blocking the way and filling the air with blinding and choking smoke.

'The Platoon worked its way through the gardens of the house and engaged the enemy at 100 yards. Major Hingston then swung 11 Platoon round and all along the combined Anglo-American front, a wild roar of small arms fire burst out. But even at this close range it was difficult to locate the foe, so effective was their concealment.'

Lance Corporal Howes was in one of the houses with B Company Headquarters, on the east-west road, and was able to watch the Americans of Company B advance on the road north of the buildings:

'The Americans were impressing us with what appeared to be both their pluck and their foolhardiness. They seemed to have no thought for personal safety and actually strolled from place to place. An American soldier would walk to the middle of the road, kneel on one knee, let off a burst or two from his automatic weapon and then walk back to cover. Of course they were having plenty of casualties.'

The Ophausen mill used as a 1/506 PIR HQ and RV for 5 DCLI.

The Church: Objective of the Anglo-American attack. The attack ground to a halt on this open ground.

PFC Garrigan was with Company B 1/506 PIR, fighting through the houses along the road:

> '*I was now a squad leader on the afternoon attack. Bill Oatman and I took off with a machine gun, jumped a couple of ditches, ran through a couple of tobacco fields with the rest of 1st Platoon with us. We finally came to a five-foot fence with the German defence on the other side – a lot of them nothing but young boys. All this time Oatman was firing his weapon and we came to a decision. We could go no further. Some of the troopers were in a house up on the road and some of them jumped the fence. The English soldiers were fighting to our left. Those who jumped the fence were never seen again.*'

A *Sturmgushutz* made a brief appearance but was driven off by accurate mortar fire. Major Hingston was wounded and wrote after the event that,

> '*I got the definite impression that things were going well and that we had won this scrap. The enemy fire was dying down and both we and our allies were still advancing and I felt that we would make the line of the church.*'

Then a message came from 1/506 PIR that their company had run out of ammunition, as they had been in action without resupply since dawn. 5 DCLI did their best to cover them back, before themselves withdrawing, also low on ammunition. The bold attack had nearly succeeded.

C Company 5 DCLI had taken a different route towards Opheusden, after becoming involved in fighting around the rail crossing and failed to follow B Company. Their alternative route north fortuitously caught Germans attempting to envelope the mill, in the flank near the southern houses of Opheusden. Had this enemy move succeeded, the Anglo-American force could have faced considerable difficulty. However, the Germans had also prevented C Company from reaching the mill and joining the attack.

Following the withdrawal of 1st Airborne Division, these Wehrmacht Sturmgeschütz photographed fighting alongside the 9th SS Panzer Division, were redeployed from Arnhem to the Island.

Reviewing the battle, Brigadier General Higgins now allocated Colonel Sink, 3/327 GIR as his regimental reserve. The 101st's historian described the decisions made:

> *'Rather than trying to squeeze this battalion into the current front line, it was decided to have it create a new defensive position 1,200 yards to the rear. Under cover of darkness the 1st Battalion, 506, and the Duke of Cornwall's Light Infantry, both badly shot up, would be withdrawn from battle. The 3rd Battalion, 506th, would fall back and take a new position as the southern portion of the newly established line. This manoeuvre would clear Allied troops out of Opheusden and leave it open for Typhoons and artillery to blast what Germans they could the next day.'*

The superior numbers of the German 363rd Division and supporting armour had succeeded in taking Opheusden. But pushing the Allied line back had taken two days of costly fighting. However, the Germans were still able to find some fresh troops with which 363rd Division could continue the battle.

Overnight, XXX Corps reorganized the defences on the Island. 50th Northumbrian Division extended its front to hold the eastern portion of the line from Driel to Bemmel and the Waal. This shortened the 101st's front considerably. 501 PIR continued to hold the Rhine front centred on Herten, while the exhausted 506 PIR was allocated the quieter Randwijk sector. 2nd and 3rd 327 GIR had taken over the western defences between the Rhine and Waal, while 502 PIR provided significant depth and reserves in the Andalst area.

Opheusden – the third day, 7 October

Before dawn, the Germans probed the new American line. At 0400 hours, they advanced across the front of Company B 1/327 GIR into a killing where Company B's fire overlapped with that of Company A's, five hundred yards away. Sergeant Ottinger was with Company B:

'This proved to be a deathtrap for the Germans. The next morning about 300 Germans started moving on Company B's flank. Lt O'Halloran waited until the Germans were about 75 yards away before he gave the order to fire. I had a BAR [Browning Automatic Rifle]. Boy, did we have a field day! What was left retreated.'

At daybreak, a fresh battalion of German infantry attacked along the railway line. This attack was well supported by artillery and mortar fire and again the attack crossed B Company's front. However, this time, rather than withering under cross fire in the five hundred yard gap between Companies A and B, the Germans successfully crossed the killing area into the rear. Heavy artillery fire had neutralized the glidermen by driving them into the cover of their foxholes. Sergeant Ottinger continued:

'Later in the morning we weren't so lucky. The enemy approached, this time with tanks. We couldn't stop all of it. Some got through. Their artillery set in and tree bursts were taking a heavy toll on us, in the apple orchard. On October 7, our company suffered 47 Casualties [almost 50% of the strength].'

However, the Germans luck was not to last, as they were heading towards depth positions where 1/506 PIR were resting. Fortunately, despite tiredness, the paratroopers' battle discipline led them to dig-in before resting. Sergeant Brininstool recalled:

'At daybreak, all hell broke loose again. We were supposedly in the back area of our own lines but not 200 yards away must have been 400 Germans. I heard a grenade explode. I jumped up, grabbed a machine gun and ran into a ditch and put the gun in action. Within minutes, all you could see was white flags. The Germans said that they had fought men of the 101st before and didn't want any more of us.'

PFC Turner recalled how the German battalion was,

'...caught in crossfire of two machine guns on 1st Battalion's perimeter. Some of us with rifles didn't bother to fire the as the machine guns were doing a good job.'

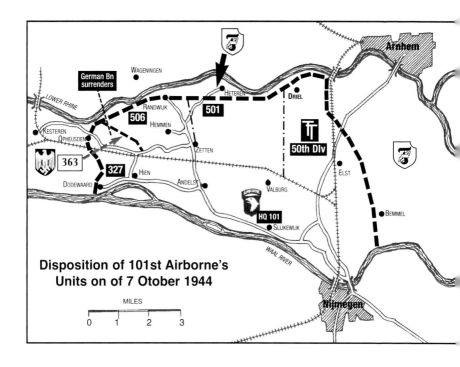

Disposition of 101st Airborne's Units on of 7 Otober 1944

Over two hundred PWs were taken and more than fifty bodies were left on the field. Company C had deployed to cut off the Germans' escape route, thus ensuring the capture of the majority of the enemy battalion.

The fighting around Opheusden continued for a further eight days. The Germans continued to press attacks from the west and across the Rhine. However, in properly prepared positions and with supplies now flowing freely up Hell's Highway, the crisis on the Island had passed.

Hard fighting continued for a succession of divisions who held the Island into the winter. Mud, the cold and wet, as well as the dominating German positions north of the Rhine reminded many older officers of their service in the Great War. The civilian population, less some stockmen and a few nuns, were evacuated from the Island when the Germans breached the dykes and flooded the plodder land.

When the Allied offensive resumed in February 1945 it did not start on the Island but from another piece of ground captured during MARKET GARDEN to the south of Nijmegen. The Island and Arnhem were not to be finally free of the enemy until April 1945.

184

CHAPTER ELEVEN

TOURS OF THE ISLAND BATTLES

This chapter contains instructions for two tours. The first tour covers the MARKET GARDEN battles that culminated in the evacuation of 1st Airborne Division and the capture of Elst, while the second tour covers the Allied engagements in late September and early October 1944.

The MARKET GARDEN Tour

This tour follows on from that in *Battleground Nijmegen* and starts in Lent on the north bank of the Waal, opposite Nijmegen. If travelling from Nijmegen, take the **Lent West** turning immediately after crossing the Bridge, turn right at the bottom of the slip road and go under the Bridge. Do not take the ramp up to the main Arnhem road but follow the local road (**Griftdijk Sud**), at the foot of the embankment, towards **Elst**. This road runs parallel to the main highway.

Following the road north out of Lent, the road passes under a railway bridge. Swinging under this bridge, on the evening of 20 September, Sergeant Robinson's troop of Grenadier Guards' Shermans, was engaged by anti-tank guns covering the road.❶ If coming south from Arnhem on the A325, take the **Lent** exit and turn right. The railway underpass is directly in front of you. This is the point reached on the evening of the seizure of the Nijmegen Bridges (see *Battleground Nijmegen*) and where the Irish Guards started their drive north the following day.

❷ Drive north towards Elst for 1.4 miles. Park in a lay-by beyond the **Oosterhout junction**. On 21 September the Irish Guards Group attempted to advance to Arnhem along this road, elevated above the surrounding countryside (see page 23). The Guards came under fire from a *Sturmguschutz* ahead of them on the road and from infantry dug-in across the fields to the right.

❸ Continue north for half a mile. Park in the area of the crossroads. 4 Wilts reached this point on the afternoon of 22 September (see page 60). This area is now built-up but beyond the houses / buildings are some large orchards. The orchards, ditches and flat open fields can be best appreciated from the car park behind the trading park a little further on.

Return towards Lent, turning right on the bend (**Zaligestraat**) just before the railway underpass. On reaching the *Oosterhout Dijk Road*, turn right towards *Oosterhout*. This is the area where 7 Som LI and 5 DCLI assembled for their attack on 22 September. Driving on along the dyke road, the 82nd US Airborne Division's monument to 504 PIR's assault crossing of the Rhine, is passed on the left (see *Battleground Nijmegen*). Continue on, passing the gate and woods surrounding *Huis Oosterhout*. This is the road taken by armoured cars of 2 HCR on the morning of 22 September. Just passed the bend is the area where the 7 Som LI and 4/7 DG came under fire from Oosterhout (see page 55) and attempted to press home their attack.

❹ The assault troops made their way to the forming up points under cover of the dyke, while the artillery bombarded the enemy positions in the village (see page 59).

Follow the route marked on the map taken by 5 DCLI during the **Dash to Driel**, via **Sijlk-Ewijk** (turn off the **Dijk Road** by the church) and **Valbourg** (see pages 9 and 64). In two places, it is not possible to follow the exact route. The first is the result of the motorway and the second is because a portion of the road leading to the **De Hoop Cross Roads** has been closed, just beyond the town's boundary sign. This necessitates a diversion. Continue into Elst, go across the roundabout and take the next left (**Vriesenek**) and drive through some new houses. Turn left and park. ❺ The **De Hoop**

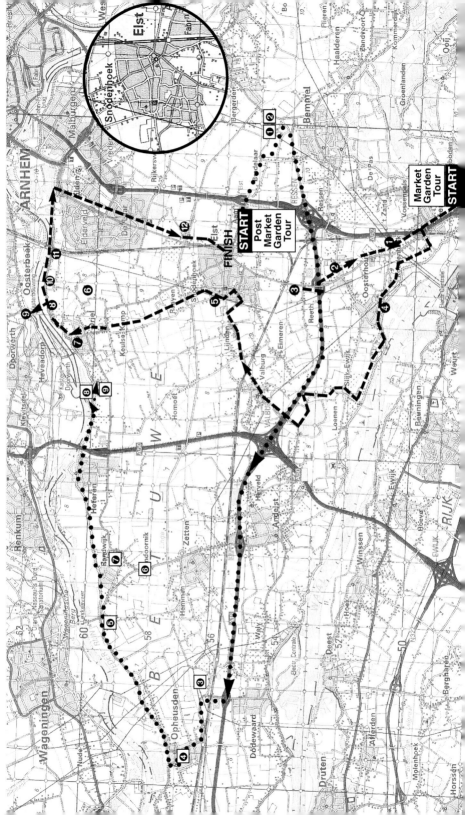

Crossroads is where the Tigers joined the armoured column and was a part of the area covered by Major Parker's tank ambush. The suburbs of Elst have expanded considerably to the west. In 1944, this area was open country on both sides of the road, with only a few houses along the road into Elst.

Continue following the Dash to Driel route, following the signs, across the Wettering Canal towards **Driel**, which 5 DCLI reached at dusk on 22 September. In the open fields to the right, is the Polish Para Brigade's DZ ❻ (see page 39). At the outskirts of **Driel** turn **right** at the T junction and then **left** on to **Dorpsraat** into **Driel**.

Little remains of wartime Driel and today the village is both larger and the buildings more numerous. Park in the **Church Square** ❼. The Church was used as an artillery OP by 112 Field Regiment and is where Generals Horrocks and Thomas came to view the situation on 23/24 September. Opposite the church, is the Polish memorial, 'symbolizing the courage and strength of the Polish nation' and bears the coats of arms of Warsaw and 1st Independent Parachute Brigade. The figure of youth represents the future and liberty. A plaque records the ninety-four Poles killed during MARKET GARDEN. The whole is as much a memorial as it is a reminder of the Cold War.

Drive through Driel onto the **Drilse Rijndijk** and turn **right** towards **Arnhem**. To the left is the River Rhine, beyond which, is the high ground north of the river, from where German observers had views across the Island that made daytime movement difficult. **Turn left** off the dyke road **down to the ferry**. Park carefully. ❽ The Poles' crossings took place five hundred yards up stream. However, this is where the Dorsets crossed on the night of 25 September (see page 81). The layout of the Rhine has changed. The original river course ends at a weir. Separated by a narrow bank of earth, a channel and lock for barges has been built. Nonetheless, the atmosphere is heavy with history, with the Westerbouwing Café / Restaurant over looking the area from the other side. It is worth **crossing the Rhine on the ferry**, which runs from spring to autumn and costs about a Pound a head.

Having crossed the ferry, walk across to the road and up the track to **Westerbouwing**. In doing so, appreciate the difficulties that 4 Dorset would have had scaling the hundred foot bluff. From the Restaurant's terrace ❾, look south to the chimneys of the Nijmegen Power Station, ten miles away. It is from there that the guns of 64 Medium Regiment, engaged targets around the Perimeter (page 35). From the terrace, a track leads westwards along the top of the bluff. It is along approximately eight hundred yards of this track that boatloads of Dorsets reached the German held woods (see page 84).

Return across the ferry to the **Drilse Rijndijk**, turn **left** and drive six hundred yards to the British and Canadian Royal Engineers Memorial ❿. Park carefully, without blocking the junction. This is the site of the evacuation of 1st Airborne Division (see page 96) on the night of 25/26 September.

Continue along the dyke road, towards the **railway embankment and bridge** ⓫. During the latter stages of MARKET GARDEN, until relief by 101st US Airborne Division, 5 Dorset held this stretch of the Rhine (see page 162). The Germans were one side of the embankment and the Allies the other, exchanging grenades. The *Sturmgeschütz* pictured on page 165 was knocked out while emerging from the underpass.

Take the Dyke Road and follow signs to the small town of Elst, which is three miles south of the river. Before reaching Elst the visitor crosses the Wettering Canal ⓬ Turn left immediately after the bridge and park on the canal bank. This is XXX Corps's high water mark on the road to Arnhem and the point held by 18 Platoon of 4 Som LI, in sight of Arnhem (see page 124).

Continue on to **Elst**, which was virtually destroyed and has been rebuilt. However, the town, with its small hotels, makes a good base for those who do not want to stay in either Arnhem or Nijmegen.

Tour of the Post MARKET GARDEN Battles

This tour starts at Elst. From the traffic lights in the centre of town, follow the signposts to the Aam factories and the Arnhem/Nijmegen motorway. Go across the railway line and **do not take** either of the turnings onto the A325. Passing the motorway slip roads, follow the local road to the right until a T junction is reached. This is the area where the Coldstream Guards' tanks supported the Dorsets' attack, which was astride the line electricity pylons (See page 148). Turn right and then left onto **Dikelsestraat**. The Dorsets forming up place is to the right and A Company 4 Dorset's objective at **De Heuvel** is to the left ❶. Passing under the first pylon line, there is a right turn (**Heuvelsestraat**), down which B Company's objective can be seen.❷ Throughout this area, most of the orchards have been removed.

As with Elst, Bemmel has expanded considerably and, at the time of writing a new road is being built across 1 Hampshires battlefield. Consequently, little understanding of the battle can be gained by attempting to follow 151 Brigade's attacks (see page 158). However, by following **Dikelestraat** onto the main **N839** and by **turning right**, the visitor is on a road that is roughly along the line of 50th Divisions objectives. To the right is Bemmel and to the left are the fields across which, the Germans were forced to withdrew to the Wettering Canal.

The other post MARKET GARDEN battles are ten miles to the west. Take a right turn signposted to **Tiel** and the **motorway**. Follow the **A15** and come off at the **Opheusden** junction. Turn right at the bottom of the slip road and park by the level crossing.

You are now on the Allied western flank, which was taken over by 101st US Airborne Division on 4 October ❸. The German 363rd Division's attack penetrated as far as this point and, for a time, denied British tanks the use of this vital rail crossing (see page 173). Cross the railway and follow the road towards **Opheusden**. This is the route forward taken by 5 DCLI before they cut across country, on the right, towards Opheusden (see page 177).

Opheusden ❹, is similar to other villages where much of the action took place in 1944, in that it was largely destroyed in the fighting and rebuilt as a modern town. However, the main road lay out is still similar and worth driving through. **Turn right** and **cross the canal** into Opheusden. This road, then as now formed the eastern edge of the village to which the Americans were pushed back (see page 173). At the end of the road is a modern church behind which stood the **Mill** (see page 177). **Turn left**. It was along this road that 5 DCLI (left) and 1/506 PIR (right) attacked towards the church. A 1940 – 1945 war memorial is on the left beyond the town hall. Turn right at the junction before reaching the church, signposted to **Rhenen**. **Turn right** on the **Rijndijk** road towards **Randwijk** and drive approximately five miles.

Two hundred yards before the ferry junction, look out for the steep turning of the dyke to the right, **Ooyhuizensestraat** ❺. C Company 7 Som LI reached orchards that used to lie at the foot of the dyke. Under cover of darkness they renewed their attacked towards the ferry that Germans were using to cross the Rhine (see page 135). A little further on is the road ❻ from the Wettering Canal that A Company used as their axis of advance to Randwijk. The crossroads ❼ held by 7 Hampshire having pushed the Germans back into the village. Return to the **Dyke Road** and continue east to **Hetren**.

The main defences of 7 Hampshire were astride the village of **Hetren**. They were subject to repeated attempts by the Germans to cross the Rhine in their extended positions (see page 139). The remains of a factory chimney can be seen on the flood plain ❽. This is the site of the factory that the Germans held for nine days. The Hampshire's memorial is located on the dyke road by a bus stop just short of **Driel** ❾.

This completes the tour of the Island battlefields. To return to Arnhem follow the dyke road until the Arnhem signs are seen. To reach Nijmegen, take a route via Driel and Elst to the A325.

XXX CORPS

HQ GUARDS ARMOURED DIVISION

N.B. Guards battalions are listed under the brigade Headquarters which they normally fought, not necessarily those to which they technically belonged.

Guards Armoured Division Signal Regiment (-)

HQ 5TH GUARDS ARMOURED BDE (*Group Hot*)

1st (Motorized) Battalion, The Grenadier Guards
2nd (Armoured) Battalion, The Grenadier Guards
1st (Armoured) Battalion, The Coldstream Guards
5th Battalion, The Coldstream Guards
55th Field Regiment Royal Artillery
14th Field Squadron Royal Engineers

HQ 32ND GUARDS ARMOURED BDE (*Group Cold*)

2nd (Armoured) Battalion, The Irish Guards
3rd Battalion, The Irish Guards
1st Battalion, The Welsh Guards
2nd (Armoured Reconnisance) Battalion, The Welsh Guards
153rd (Leicestershire Yeomanry) Field Regiment Royal Artillery
615th Field Squadron Royal Engineers

GUARDS ARMOURED DIVISIONAL TROOPS

HQ 21st Anti-Tank Regiment Royal Artillery
HQ 94th Light Anti-Aircraft Regiment Royal Artillery
HQ Guards Armoured Division Engineer Regiment, Field Park
Company 11th Bridging Troop RE and Divisional Postal Unit
1st Independent Machine gun Company, The Royal Northumberland Fusiliers
Royal Army Service Corps HQ Guards Armoured Division RASC
Battalion, Tank Delivery Squadron
Royal Army Medical Corps 19th Light Field Ambulance, 128th Field
Ambulance and Field Hygiene Section
Royal Army Ordnance Corps Guards Armoured Division Ordnance Field Park, Company RAOC + Mobile Bath Unit
Royal Electrical and Mechanical Engineers 5th Guards Armoured
Brigade Workshop, 32nd Guards Armoured Brigade Workshop
Military Police Guards Armoured Division Company Royal Corps of Military Police
Intelligence Corps Field Security Section

43rd WESSEX DIVISION

HQ 43rd (WESSEX) INFANTRY DIVISION

43rd (Wessex) Divisional Signals Regiment

HQ 129th INFANTRY BRIGADE

4th Battalion, The Somerset Light Infantry
4th Battalion, The Wiltshire Regiment
5th Battalion, The Wiltshire Regiment

94th (Dorset and Hampshire) Field Regiment Royal Artillery
235th Anti-Tank Battery
206th Field Company Royal Engineers
A (Machine gun) Company 8th Middlesex (including a Heavy Mortar Platoon)
129th Field Ambulance
Support Troop 360th Light AA Battery
30th Independent Anti-Aircraft Troop
2nd Company Divisional Signal Regiment
504th Company Royal Army Service Corps

HQ 130th INFANTRY BRIGADE

7th Battalion, The Hampshire Regiment
4th Battalion, The Dorsetshire Regiment
5th Battalion, The Dorsetshire Regiment
112th (Wessex) Field Regiment Royal Artillery
233rd Anti-Tank Battery
553rd Field Company Royal Engineers
B (Machine gun) Company 8th Middlesex (including a Heavy Mortar Platoon)
130th Field Ambulance
Support Troop 362nd Light AA Battery
32nd Independent Anti-Aircraft Troop
3rd Company 43rd Divisional Signals Regiment
505th Company Royal Army Service Corps

HQ 214th INFANTRY BRIGADE

7th Battalion Somerset Light Infantry
1st Battalion The Worcestershire Regiment
5th Battalion Duke of Cornwall's Light Infantry
179th Field Regiment Royal Artillery
333rd Anti-Tank Battery Royal Artillery
204th Field Company Royal Engineers
C (Machine gun) Company 8th Middlesex (including a Heavy Mortar Platoon)
213th Field Ambulance
Support Troop 361st Light Anti-Aircraft Battery
31st Independent Anti-Aircraft Troop
4th Company 43rd Divisional Signal Regiment
54th Company Royal Army Service Corps

43rd WESSEX DIVISIONAL TROOPS

43rd Reconnisance Regiment
HQ 59th Anti-Tank (Gloucesters) Regiment Royal Artillery and 236th Battery
HQ 110th Light Anti-Aircraft Regiment RA (7th Dorsets), 360th Battery (-), 361st Battery (-) and 362nd Battery (-) HQ 43rd Division Engineers
Regiment, 207th Field Park Company and 43rd Divisional Postal Unit
HQ 8th (Machine gun) Battalion, The Middlesex Regiment
Royal Army Service Corps HQ 43rd Division RAOC Battalion and 506th Company RAOC
Royal Army Medical Corps 14th Field Dressing Section, 15th Field Dressing Section and 38th Field Hygiene Section
Royal Army Ordnance Corps 43rd Division Ordnance Field Park and 306th Mobile Bath Unit
Royal Electrical and Mechanical Engineers

129th Infantry Brigade Workshop, 130th
Infantry Brigade Workshop and 214th
Infantry Brigade Workshop
Military Police 43rd Division Company Royal
Corps of Military Police
Intelligence Corps 57th Field Security Section

50th NORTHUMBRIAN DIVISION

HQ 50th NORTHUMBRIAN DIVISION
50th Northumbrian Divisional Signals Regiment (-)
69th INFANTRY BRIGADE
5th Battalion The East Yorkshire Regiment
1st Battalion The Green Howards
7th Battalion The Green Howards
bbth Field Regiment Royal Artillery
99th Anti-Tank Battery Royal Artillery
233rd Field Company Royal Engineers
B (Machine gun) Company 2nd Cheshire (including
a Heavy Mortar Platoon)
149th Field Ambulance
Support Troop nnst Light Anti-Aircraft Battery
2nd Company 50th Divisional Signal Regiment
Brigade Company Royal Army Service Corps
151st INFANTRY BRIGADE
6th Battalion The Durham Light Infantry
8th Battalion The Durham Light Infantry
9th Battalion The Durham Light Infantry
bbth Field Regiment Royal Artillery
289th Anti-Tank Battery Royal Artillery
505th Field Company Royal Engineers
A (Machine gun) Company 2nd Cheshire (including
a Heavy Mortar Platoon)
186th Field Ambulance
Support Troop Light Anti-Aircraft Battery
3rd Company 50th Divisional Signal Regiment
Brigade Company Royal Army Service Corps

231st (MALTA) INFANTRY BRIGADE
2nd Battalion, The Devonshire Regiment
1st Battalion, The Dorsetshire Regiment
1st Battalion, The Hampshire Regiment
90th Field Regiment Royal Artillery
282nd Anti-Tank Battery Royal Artillery
295th Field Company Royal Engineers
C (Machinegun) Company 2nd Cheshire (including
a Heavy Mortar Platoon)
186th Field Ambulance
Support Troop Light Anti-Aircraft Battery
3rd Company 50th Divisional Signal Regiment
Brigade Company Royal Army Service Corps

50th NORTHUMBRIAN DIVISIONAL TROOPS
61st Reconnaissance Regiment
HQ 102nd (Northumberland Hussars) Anti-Tank
Regiment Royal Artillery, 107 Battery
HQ 25th Light Anti-Aircraft Regiment, hh Battery (-
), bb Battery (-) and kkd Battery (-)
HQ 50th Division Engineers Regiment, 235rd Field
Park Company and 50th Divisional Postal Unit
HQ 2nd (Machine gun) Battalion, The Cheshire
Regiment
Royal Army Service Corps HQ 50th Division
RAOC Battalion and cc Company RAOC

Royal Army Medical Corps 47th Field Dressing
Section, 48th Field Dressing Section and 22nd
Field Hygiene Section
Royal Army Ordnance Corps 50th Division
Ordnance Field Park and Mobile Bath Unit
Royal Electrical and Mechanical Engineers 69th
Infantry Brigade
Workshop, 151st Infantry Brigade Workshop and
231st Infantry Brigade Workshop
Military Police 50th Division Company Royal Corps
of Military Police
Intelligence Corps Field Security Section

8th ARMOURED BRIGADE
Brigade Headquarters and Signal Squadron
4th/7th Dragoon Guards
13th/18th Hussars
Nottinghamshire (Sherwood Rangers) Yeomanry
12th Battalion, King's Royal Rifle Corps
147th (Essex Yeomanry) Field Regiment Royal
Artillery
8th Armoured Brigade Workshop

101st US
AIRBORNE DIVISION

HEADQUARTERS 101ST US AIRBORNE Division
101st Signal Company and 101st Headquarter
Company
501st PARACHUTE INFANTRY REGIMENT
1st Battalion, 501st Parachute Infantry Regt
2nd Battalion, 501st Parachute Infantry Regt
3rd Battalion, 501st Parachute Infantry Regt
502nd PARACHUTE INFANTRY REGIMENT
1st Battalion, 502nd Parachute Infantry Regt
2nd Battalion, 502nd Parachute Infantry Regt
3rd Battalion, 502nd Parachute Infantry Regt
506th PARACHUTE INFANTRY REGIMENT
1st Battalion, 506th Parachute Infantry Regt
2nd Battalion, 506th Parachute Infantry Regt
3rd Battalion, 506th Parachute Infantry Regt
327th GLIDER INFANTRY REGIMENT
1st Battalion, 327th Glider Infantry Regt
2nd Battalion, 327th Glider Infantry Regt
3rd Battalion (formerly 1st Battalion, 401st)
Glider Infantry Regt
DIVISIONAL TROOPS
101st Parachute Maintenance Battalion
326th Airborne Engineer Battalion
326th Airborne Medical Company
81st Airborne Anti-aircraft and Anti-tank Battalion
321st Glider Field Artillery Battalion
377th Parachute Field Artillery Battalion
907th Glider Field Artillery Battalion
801st Ordnance Company
426th Quartermaster Company
397th Quartermaster Truck Company
101st Military Police Platoon
101st Reconnaissance Platoon